THE

# POETICAL WORKS

OF

## EDGAR ALLAN POE,

*COMPLETE.*

WITH MEMOIR AND VINDICATION.

NEW YORK:
W. J. WIDDLETON, PUBLISHER.
1876

# BIOGRAPHICAL SKETCH OF EDGAR A. POE.

THE story of Poe's life is briefly as follows: He was the son of David and Elizabeth (Arnold) Poe, and was born at Boston in February, 1809. Mrs. Poe died deserted and in poverty at Richmond in December, 1811. Edgar was adopted by Mr. John Allan, a Richmond merchant, who was a kind-hearted and indulgent man,—the last person in the world who should have had the care of such a child. In 1816 the Allans travelled in England, Scotland, and Ireland, and placed their adopted child at school at Stoke Newington, near London, where, under Dr. Bransby, he remained five or six years, at the end of which time he returned to America and lived again with the Allan family at Richmond, where he continued his studies for three or four years under the best masters that could be obtained. In 1826 he entered the University of Virginia, which at that time was a most dissolute place. Poe did not escape the temptations of the place, although the record of his scholarship is good, for he was a more than ordinarily apt pupil. He remained at college from February to December, 1826, spending a large amount of money—for Mr. Allan was rich and indulgent to him—and running in debt some two thousand dollars. Most of his money was lost in gambling, which was a perfect mania with the students of the college.

On leaving the university, he remained with the Allans, and in 1829 published his first book, "Al Aaraaf, Tamerlane, and Minor Poems." It had no great success, and Poe looked about him for a career unconnected with literature. He secured admission as a cadet at West Point; but, learning of his foster-father's second marriage, decided that the army was unfitted for a man who would be independent, took measures, contrary to Mr. Allan's wishes, to get a discharge from the academy, in which efforts he finally succeeded. He was at his wit's end as to what he should do. He had expected to be Mr. Allan's heir, but his adoptive father had now a child of his own; and Edgar's disobedience of his expressed wish, that he should remain at West Point, completely estranged him from Mr. Allan. He published another collection of poems, which was not more successful than the first; and then for a number of years all reliable trace of him is lost, until 1833, when he is again found in Baltimore. The proprietors of the "Saturday Visitor" offered two prizes,— one for the best tale and one for the best poem that should be sent to them. Poe submitted a poem and six prose sketches, and was the successful competitor. He was then very poor, and had been ill, but his fortunes brightened, and his stories in the "Southern Literary Messenger" attracted much attention. In 1835 he accepted an editorial position on the Messenger, and removed to Richmond, where it was published; but in 1837 his connection with the periodical was severed, and about the same time he married his cousin, Virginia Clemm. In 1839 he became editor of Mr. William E. Burton's "Gentleman's Magazine" at a salary of ten dollars a week. It was in this magazine that the finest of his tales,

"The Fall of the House of Usher," first appeared, as also did the strange story "William Wilson." In 1840 his connection with the magazine ceased, and when "Graham's Magazine" was established Poe was the editor, a position which he did not long hold, being succeeded by Dr. Griswold. In 1844 he was employed on the New York "Mirror," shortly afterwards on the "Broadway Journal," and in 1845 on the "American Review," in which "The Raven" appeared. He became editor and proprietor of the "Broadway Journal," which he ran on his principle that "the people love havoc," and after the death of which, in 1846, he wrote a number of criticisms on the "Literati of New York" for the "Lady's Book," in which his irritable nerves commonly did the work which should have been left to his intellect for its accomplishment; for although many of his expressed views are perfectly correct, the injustice of many of them is apparent on the mere reading, though the reader has never read the writings which gave occasion for them.

The good work that he had done had by this time given him a European reputation sufficiently important to warrant a review of his writings in the "Revue des Deux Mondes," and he was, as Mr. Stoddard says, a celebrity. He was poor, however, not because he did not write well, but partly because of his habits, and mainly because he wrote too well to command prices at all commensurate with the amount of labor he bestowed on his work. For instance, he received ten dollars for "The Raven," and if the price commanded by his other writings was proportionate to this, it may readily be seen why he was poor. While living at Fordham he and his wife were both ill, and in such terrible want that through the kindness of Mr. Willis, then editor of the "Home Journal," a subscription was raised for them which temporarily relieved their embarrassments.

In 1848 his beloved and loving wife, Virginia, died, and he did no work for some time except "Eureka: A Prose Poem," in which he attempted to solve the problem of the universe, as Griswold — perhaps as incompetent a man as ever lived to talk about such matters — says, according to the "exploded theories of 'The Vestiges of Creation.'" In the same year he lectured in public, delivering a lecture entitled "The Poetic Principle." In 1849 "The Bells" and "Annabel Lee" appeared; and in the summer he left Fordham intending to go to Richmond, but stopped at Philadelphia, where, meeting some of his old companions, he was tempted to drink, spent all his money, and at last, through the kindness of old friends, reached his destination, where, obtaining desk-room at the office of a friend, he engaged in literary pursuits for a while, and then suddenly disappeared to return again and disappear again, his malady of drink ever torturing him and disturbing his best endeavors. He tried to reform, joined a temperance society, lectured on temperance, and was received by the best people of Richmond. Here he met a lady whom he had loved in early life and became engaged to marry her. He started for home to attend to some business matters and fetch Mrs. Clemm, his mother-in-law, to his wedding. He stopped at Baltimore, drank with a friend, was taken from Havre de Grace, a way-station, back to Baltimore, still prostrated by the effects of liquor, of which, delicately constituted as he was, he could not drink a single glass without losing all control over himself. In this state, he fell into the hands of the political harpies known as the "Dead Rabbits," a society of repeaters. By them he was "cooped," confined in a room at the political headquarters, taken from there through the open streets in the midst of a heavy storm to the various voting offices, and then drugged again, and left exhausted and nearly dead from the exposure.

The effect of this outrage upon his delicate constitution was to bring on a return of the malady from which he had suffered two years before, which in this case, aggravated by the effects of the powerful drugs that had been administered, proved fatal, and he died on the 7th of October, 1849, after an illness of a few days, at the hospital in Baltimore, surrounded by the few relatives and friends who could be notified in season to minister to him in his last moments.

# EDGAR A. POE AND HIS BIOGRAPHER.

# Edgar A. Poe and his Biographer.

A Vindication of Poe from the Aspersions of Rufus W. Griswold.

BY WILLIAM F. GILL.

"Dr. Griswold's biography of my Eddie is one atrocious lie," writes Mrs. Clemm, the mother-in-law of Edgar Allan Poe, in a letter to an intimate friend; and after careful researches, extending over the space of three years, I have come, from the cumulation of corroborative documentary evidence, to give an unequivocal endorsement to Mrs. Clemm's statement. Intense admiration of Poe's writings and of his genius, mingled with deep sympathy for the exceptional misfortunes of his career, first prompted me to the arduous task of investigating the story of his life, and verifying or disproving the statements of the Griswold biography of Poe, which for nearly twenty-five years has been permitted to preface the authorized editions of his works, also forming the basis of several of the biographies that have been written to preface the English editions of the poet's works. As a matter of fact, Poe's poems are five-fold more popular in England than in America, and his prose writings, which have never secured the recognition of extended popular currency in America, are even more admired in England than are his poems. I cannot refrain from feeling and expressing the conviction that Griswold's mendacious biography, preluding the American editions of Poe, and, as it were, forming a chilling wet-blanket, most repelling to the warmest admirer of the poet, is in a degree responsible for the comparatively limited circulation enjoyed by his works in America. I measure the effect of the Griswold biography upon the intelligent reader precisely as does an English reviewer the biography of Poe by James Hannay, based upon Griswold, to wit: Should any man of taste and sense, not acquainted with Poe, be so unfortunate as to look at Mr. Griswold's preface before reading the poetry, it is extremely probable he will throw the book into the fire, in indignation at the self-conceit and affected smartness by which the preface is characterized.

As a matter of fact, the demand for the complete edition of Poe's works containing the Griswold memoir, is so limited that, within a few months, calling for this edition at two of the largest book-houses in Boston, I was unable to obtain a copy, and was informed that the calls for it were so few that they, the dealers, were not encouraged to keep this edition of Poe in stock. Yet no one will deny that among the *collections* of poems by various authors published, Poe is among the most popular and the most admired of the authors represented.

My purpose in this paper being to offer an impartial statement, or a series of statements, duly authenticated by documents, controverting the statements of Dr. Griswold, rather than to attempt any eulogium of the poet, I shall devote my allotted space, so far as it will allow, principally to meeting the misstatements of the reverend vilifier. Some of Dr. Griswold's statements are properly attributable to malicious and vengeful mendacity, others to gross and inexcusable carelessness. *Imprimis*, the biographer states that Edgar A. Poe was born in Baltimore, January, 1811. Mr. Poe was not born in 1811, in Baltimore, but in 1809, in Boston; this is on the authority of the records (still in existence) of the University of Virginia, at Charlottesville.

"In 1816," writes the biographer, "he accompanied Mr. and Mrs. Allan to Great Britain, and afterwards passed four or five years in a school kept at Stoke Newington, near London, by the Rev. Dr. Bransby." "Encompassed by the massy walls of this venerable academy" (writes the poet in "William Wilson"), "I passed, yet not in tedium or disgust, the years of the third lustrum of my life." Had he not been born until 1811, as Dr. Griswold states, he would not have attained his third lustrum during his sojourn at this place.

Of this school and its playground Poe writes in the same sketch: "The extensive enclosure was irregular in form, having many capacious recesses. Of these, three or four of the largest constituted the playground. It was level and covered with hard gravel. . . . But the house, how quaint an old building was this! to me how veritably a palace of enchantment! There was really no end to its windings, to its incomprehensible subdivisions. It was difficult at any given time to say with certainty upon which of its two stories one happened to be. From each room to every other there were sure to be found three or four steps either in ascent or descent.

"Then the lateral branches were innumerable, inconceivable, and so returning in upon themselves that our most exact ideas in regard to the whole mansion were not very far different from those with which we pondered upon infinity. During the five years of my residence here I was never able to ascertain with precision in what remote locality lay the little sleeping apartment assigned to myself and some eighteen or twenty other scholars."

"In 1822" (continues Dr. Griswold) "he entered the university at Charlottesville, Virginia, where he led a very dissipated life. The manners which then prevailed there were extremely dissolute, and he was known as the wildest and most reckless student of his class; but his unusual opportunities, and the remarkable ease with which he mastered the most difficult studies, kept him all the while in the first rank for scholarship, and he would have graduated with the highest honors had not his gambling, intemperance, and other vices induced his expulsion from the university."

This is all false from beginning to end, and is absurd, likewise, on the biographer's own showing. If Poe was born in 1811, he would at this time (1822) have been *eleven* years of age, — rather a precocious age, is it not, for one to whom is ascribed the rôle of a rake and a gambler? As a matter of fact, Poe did not enter the university until 1826, being then just seventeen years of age. He was never, according to reliable evidence, intoxicated while there, nor was he expelled.

Following the death of his foster-father, there came to Poe a period of great, although probably not of his greatest, suffering. He had not at that time secured attention as a writer, and his condition and location up to the time of his appearance as a competitor for the Baltimore prizes are veiled from his biographers. It is not improbable, however, that he made his headquarters at the time with his aunt, Mrs. Clemm, who afterwards became his mother-in-law. Dr. Griswold, not having a fact at hand to mortise into this gap, comes to the rescue of his impotent researches, and as usual placidly *invents* another bit of defamatory fiction. "His contributions," says Dr. Griswold, "attracted little attention, and his hopes of gaining a living in this way being disappointed, he enlisted in the army as a private soldier. How long he remained in the army I have not been able to ascertain. He was recognized by officers who had known him at West Point, and efforts were made privately, but with prospects, to obtain for him a commission, when it was discovered by his friends that he had deserted." The facts are, on the written testimony of Mrs. Clemm, that at this time his friends were seeking for him a commission, and it is folly to believe, when the prospects were favorable for his securing a higher position, that he would have enlisted as a private, and thus deliberately and unnecessarily have incurred the penalty and disgrace of desertion. That Mrs. Clemm, at least, was in full knowledge of his whereabouts at this time, is evident from her statement made in this regard, that Poe never slept one night away from home until after he was married. It is futile to say that such an audacious rumor should never have obtained admission into a memoir of Poe, and that it never would have done so had proper inquiries been made. Griswold never cared to make inquiries, and if he had, he was in his normal condition too unclean a man ever to have made *proper* inquiries.

Dr. Griswold's next fabrication is in regard to the details of Poe's appearance as a competitor for the prizes offered by the proprietor of the "Saturday Visitor" at Baltimore. The prizes were one for the best tale and one for the best poem. Dr. Griswold states that, attracted by the beauty of Poe's penmanship, the committee, without opening any of the other manuscripts, voted unanimously that the prizes should be paid to "the first of geniuses who had written legibly." On the contrary, there appeared in the "Visitor," after the awards were made, complimentary comments over the committee's own signatures. They said, among other things, that *all* the tales offered by Poe were far *better than the best* offered by others, adding "that they thought it a duty to call public attention to them in these columns in that marked manner, since they possessed a singular force and beauty, and were eminently distinguished by a rare, vigorous, and poetical imagination, a rich style, a fertile invention, and varied and curious learning."

It is not a matter of great importance, but Dr. Griswold's famous pen-photograph of Poe's personal appearance when summoned by Mr. Kennedy to receive his prize-money, is also untrue. I have not the copy of the letter at hand, and therefore cannot recall the precise words of Mr. Kennedy; but I have in my possession a copy of an original letter, which most positively states that Poe's appearance, although somewhat shabby, was not by any means absolutely poverty-stricken, and that the details of the absence of shirt and stockings, mentioned by Dr. Griswold, are false. This statement is interesting as, in a way, confirmatory of my impression that Poe was not so far reduced as he has been represented at this time. And when it is remembered that there is evidence that he had influential friends at that very time working to secure a commission for him, is it probable that they would have permitted him to go about in such a shocking condition as has been represented? The theory that he was at this time living with friends, is palpably more probable.

That his success in securing the prizes decided him upon enlisting in a literary career, there can be no doubt; hence it is a matter of no surprise that we hear no more of the army project at this time.

From other data, which have come to me from private sources, I learn that he met Virginia Clemm when she was but six years of age, that he undertook her tuition at ten, and married her when she was but fourteen. From this it is again not only evident, but undoubted, that he was at least a frequent visitor at the Clemms' at the period of his career about which so little is known to the world. An amusing instance of Griswold's pettiness and want of common-sense judgment, even in his endeavor to demean the position and character of his subject as much as possible, is found in the following paragraph in the biography. Speaking of the poet's connection with the "Literary Messenger," he writes, "In the next number of the "Messenger," Mr. White announced that Poe was its editor, or, in other words, that he had made arrangements with a gentleman of approved literary taste and attainments, to whose especial management the editorial department would be confided, and it was declared that this gentleman would 'devote his exclusive attention to his work.'" Having put this down in black and white, following his statement that Mr. White was a man of much purity of character, the redoubtable biographer evidently feels that he has set Poe up a peg too high, and immediately planes him down to an endurable level in the next sentence: "Poe continued, however, to reside in Baltimore, and it is probable that he was engaged only as a *general contributor* and *writer of critical notices of books.*" Apropos of these book reviews, Dr. Griswold dismisses them as follows: "He continued in Baltimore till September. In this period he wrote several long reviews, which for the most part were abstracts of works rather than critical discussions." As a matter of fact, the "Messenger" was in its seventh month, with about four hundred subscribers, when Poe assumed the editorship. Poe remained with this journal until the end of its second year, by which time its circulation had been increased fourfold. A contemporary of Poe writes that "the success of the Messenger has been justly attributable to Poe's exertions on its behalf, but especially to the skill, honesty, and audacity of the criticism under the editorial head. The review of 'Norman Leslie' may be said to have introduced a new era in our critical literature." But Griswold could see nothing in Poe's book reviews of which he cared to speak, for reasons which will be apparent later.

Dr. Griswold's next mendacious allusion to Poe is in connection with his account of his secession from the "Gentleman's Magazine."

After mentioning a personal correspondence between Burton and Poe, in which the views of the latter, whatever they may have been, are carefully suppressed, Dr. Griswold romances as follows: "He [Burton] was absent nearly a fortnight, and on returning he found that his printers had not received a line of copy, but that Poe had prepared the prospectus of a new monthly, and obtained transcripts of his subscription and account books, to be used in a scheme for supplanting him. He encountered his associate late in the evening at one of his accustomed haunts, and said, 'Mr. Poe, I am astonished. Give me my manuscripts, so that I can attend to the duties which you have so shamefully neglected, and when you are sober we will settle.' Poe interrupted him with, 'Who are you that presume to address me in this manner? Burton, I am the editor of the "Pennsylvania Magazine," and you are — hiccup — a *fool!*' Of course, this ended his relations with the 'Gentleman's.'" That this alleged conversation, so plausibly narrated as to pass current *nem. con.*, were it not for the existence of more reliable documentary evidence, is an audacious invention, has been made apparent to me from the written testimony of gentlemen connected with the "Gentleman's Magazine" at this time.

Dr. Griswold devotes considerable space to his next misstatement, which relates to Mr. Poe's reading of an original poem before the Boston Lyceum. Our lecture managers and lecture public were more exacting twenty-five years ago, on some points, than at the present time. *Now*, it suffices for a reputable celebrity to *show* himself upon the rostrum. Provided he does not occupy too much time (one hour or an hour and fifteen minutes is about the fashionable limit), he may be sure of copious applause, of fervent congratulations from beaming managers, and a plethoric purse upon retiring. *Then*, O insatiable manager and exacting public! the best literary work expressly performed for the occasion was demanded, or woe betide the celebrities who failed to meet these requirements!

Poe was probably fully conscious of this, and, not unlike other geniuses in the history of the literary world, was driven wellnigh frantic in contemplation of his task of the "written-expressly-for-this-occasion poem." It ended as most of these unequal contests between inspiration and necessity have ended time and time again. The day arrived, and no new creations had been evolved from the goaded and temporarily irresponsive brain. He went to Boston to fill his engagement, nerved to meet the ordeal by a spirit which brought him compensation for his anxiety,—a spirit which Mr. E. P. Whipple, the distinguished essayist, at that time immediately associated with Poe, most admirably describes as intellectual mischief.*

* Poe's connection with the Text-Book of Conchology, of which Dr. Griswold makes such a point, is undoubtedly attributable to this same spirit of intellectual mischief. No other cause can reasonably be assigned for the publication of the

He could not do what he had been invited to do: well, he would make them believe that he had filled the demand, if he could, and then honestly own up, and let them laugh at him and with him.

Dr. Griswold makes a labored effort to show that Poe's failure to meet his engagement to the letter was due to cares, anxieties, and "feebleness of will." The charge of feebleness of will, applied to Poe in his strictly literary capacity, is perhaps one of the most sapient bits of analysis of which the reverend and profound doctor has delivered himself. As regards Dr. Griswold's mention of the assistance of Mrs. Osgood, desired by Poe, it is so manifestly absurd that the biographer's ingenuity and invention fail to enlist any credence in this bit of fiction.

The literary world of Boston twenty-five years ago was marked by characteristics that rendered it anything but liberal and indulgent. Had Poe had the fortunate tact to disarm his audience by "owning up" at the outset, and in advance, deftly knuckling, as he might have done, to its boasted literary acumen and perceptiveness, all might have been well. But he chose rather to indulge his mischievous propensity, to his cost, as it afterwards proved. In his card in the "Broadway Journal," the poet, in acknowledging his confession to a company of gentlemen at a supper which took place after the reading, truly says, in closing, "We should have waited a couple of days." He should indeed have waited; for among the company was a pitcher that could not contain the water, and the premature leak, being made public, naturally aroused a storm of indignant criticism upon the poet's

book under the circumstances. There was no money in such a venture, and the action partakes so much of the color of Poe's purely mischievous pranks in other fields that I cannot but assign it to the same species of impulse.

assumption. His long poem had been applauded to the echo, and the reading of "The Raven" afterwards had sent the audience home in the best of spirits. Poe was too frank and impulsive to keep the joke to himself, and, finding that he had not taken in *all* of the men with brains who received him, he, without a word of suggestion, made a clean breast of it. How did the truth get to the papers? is the question. We were young indeed, then, it is true. But must not the full-fledged interviewer of the present day have been a grub at some time? and, if so, may not he then have lain snugly ensconced in the comfortable folds of Poe's black frock?

It is difficult to meet with absolute documentary evidence such a statement as Griswold makes in regard to the poet borrowing money of a lady, and then, when asked to return it as promised, threatening to exhibit a correspondence that would make the woman infamous. Griswold manages, however, to admit that whatever his subject might have been with men, he was "*different*" with women; and the numerous letters which I have seen in the poet's hand to the select circle of his near lady friends mark his relations with them as characterized by uniform delicacy, deference, and chaste feeling. That this glittering generality of Griswold's, in this instance of the borrowing, is another glaring falsehood, every known attribute of the poet tends to show.

As regards Mr. Poe's letters alluding to his dangerous illness, concerning which Mr. Griswold states that Poe was not dangerously ill at all at the time, I have the testimony of a most estimable lady now living, at whose house Mr. Poe was a frequent visitor, that Mr. Poe was almost at death's door at the time from an attack of congestion of the brain, which was in reality the final cause of his death. I have also the testimony before me in Mr. Poe's own hand, spite of Griswold's statement that there was no literary or personal abuse of him in the journals of which Poe complained, that at this very time he (Poe) brought a suit for libel against one of his vilifiers and obtained "exemplary damages."

Speaking of the severing of Poe's connection with "Graham's Magazine," Dr. Griswold writes, "The infirmities which induced his separation from Mr. White and Mr. Burton at length compelled Mr. Graham to find another editor"; and also in the same connection, "It is known that the personal ill-will on both sides was such that for some four or five years *not a line by Poe was purchased for* 'Graham's Magazine.'" The italics are Dr. Griswold's. He evidently believes with Chrysos, the art-patron in W. S. Gilbert's play of "Pygmalion and Galatea," that when a person tells a lie he "should tell it well."

It is a patent fact that, among the indignant refutations of Griswold's mendacious memoir of Poe, which was published both in newspaper and magazine form previous to its being included with Poe's works, was a manly and spirited defence of the poet written by Mr. Graham in the "New York Tribune." Mr. Graham, a few months later, wrote in his own magazine a more extended review of Griswold's memoir, from which we append the following significant extracts: "I knew Mr. Poe well,—far better than Mr. Griswold; and, by the memory of old times when he was an editor of 'Graham's,' I pronounce this exceedingly ill-timed and unappreciative estimate of our lost friend *unfair* and *untrue*. It is Mr. Poe as seen by the writer while laboring under a fit of the nightmare; but so dark a picture has no resemblance to the living man. It must have been made in a moment of spleen, written out and laid aside, and handed to the printer, when his death was announced, with a sort of a chuckle. He is not Mr. Poe's peer, and I challenge him before the country even as a juror in the case."

Of the parallel drawn between Poe and Bulwer's Francis Vivian in "The Caxtons," in which Dr. Griswold paints in lurid colors the alleged envy and vaulting ambition of the poet, Mr. Graham writes, "Now, this is dastardly, and, what is worse, it is false. It is very adroitly done, with phrases very well turned, and with gleams of truth shining out from a setting so dusky as to look devilish. Mr. Griswold does not feel the worth of the man he has undervalued, he has no sympathies in common with him, and has allowed old prejudices and old enmities to steal, insensibly perhaps, into the coloring of his picture. They were for years totally uncongenial, if not enemies; and during that period Mr. Poe, in a scathing lecture upon 'Poets of America,' gave Griswold some raps over the knuckles of force sufficient to be remembered.

"Nor do I consider Mr. Griswold *competent*, with all the opportunities he may have cultivated or acquired, to act as his judge; to dissect that subtile and singularly fine intellect, to probe the motives and weigh the actions of that proud heart. His whole nature — that distinctive presence of the departed which now stands impalpable, yet in strong outline before me, as I knew him and *felt* him to be — eludes the rude grasp of a mind so warped and uncongenial as Mr. Griswold's."

This statement of Mr. Graham's was in the form of an open letter to Mr. N. P. Willis, and carefully avoided any specific personal charges, demonstrating more exactly the basis of Dr. Griswold's unscrupulous and malignant animus. As Dr. Griswold never presumed to make any detailed public reply to this or similar articles derogatory to the fairness of his views, it is perhaps as well that the more specific charges that might have been made have been reserved for the present time.

Mr. Graham is now living, and when I last saw him he was in excellent health. I was then, of course, intent upon securing data in regard to the life of Poe, and in a conversation with Mr. Graham some peculiarly significant facts touching Griswold's veracity in particular were elicited.

Mr. Graham states that Poe never quarrelled with him, never was *discharged* from "Graham's Magazine"; and that during the "four or five years" italicized by Dr. Griswold as indicating the personal ill-will between Mr. Poe and Mr. Graham, over *fifty* articles by Poe were accepted by Mr. Graham.

The facts of Mr. Poe's secession from "Graham's" were as follows: —

Mr. Poe was, from illness or other causes, absent for a short time from his post on the magazine. Mr. Graham had, meanwhile, made a temporary arrangement with Dr. Griswold to act as Poe's substitute until his return. Poe came back unexpectedly, and, seeing Griswold in his chair, turned on his heel without a word, and left the office, nor could he be persuaded to enter it again, although, as stated, he sent frequent contributions thereafter to the pages of the magazine.

The following anecdote well illustrates the character of Poe's biographer. Dr. Griswold's associate in his editorial duties on "Graham's" was Mr. Charles J. Peterson, a gentleman long and favorably known in connection with prominent American magazines. Jealous of his abilities, and unable to visit his vindictiveness upon him *in propria persona*, Dr. Griswold conceived the noble design of stabbing him in the back, writing under a *nom de plume* in another journal, the

"New York Review." In the columns of the "Review" there appeared a most scurrilous attack upon Mr. Peterson, at the very time in the daily interchange of friendly courtesies with his treacherous associate. Unluckily for Dr. Griswold, Mr. Graham saw this article, and, immediately inferring, from its tone, that Griswold was the undoubted author, went to him with the article in his hand, saying, "Dr. Griswold, I am very sorry to say I have detected you in what I call a piece of rascality." Griswold turned all colors upon seeing the article, but stoutly denied the imputation, saying, "I 'll go before an alderman and swear that I never wrote it." It was fortunate that he was not compelled to add perjury to his meanness, for Mr. Graham said no more about the matter at that time, waiting his opportunity for authoritative confirmation of the truth of his surmises. He soon found his conjectures confirmed to the letter. Being well acquainted with the editor of the "Review," he took occasion to call upon him shortly afterwards when in New York. Asking as a special favor to see the manuscript of the article in question, it was handed to him. The writing was in Griswold's hand.

Returning to Philadelphia, he called Griswold to him, told him the facts, paid him a month's salary in advance, and dismissed him from his post on the spot.

So it becomes evident that the memory of Poe's biographer, confused upon the point of his discharge from "Graham's," has saddled Poe with the humiliation and disgrace that alone belonged to him. The probing of the personal history of Rufus W. Griswold is like stirring up a jar of sulphuretted hydrogen, — it exhales nothing but foul and loathsome odors. Most of the associations of this man in private life are too vile to place before refined readers. One anecdote I may be permitted to give, to illustrate his utter heartlessness and depravity.

At one time in his career he met and became well acquainted with two ladies (sisters) from South Carolina, who were reputed to be very wealthy. He paid them every attention, and finally became engaged to one of them, whom he shortly afterwards married. On the very day of the wedding, and almost immediately after the ceremony, he was informed that the estimable lady whom he had made his wife was a portionless bride. There had been no attempt made by the lady to create the impression that she was wealthy, nor did she dream for a moment that a supposed fortune, and not herself, had secured the villain's attachment. Dr. Griswold made short work of sentiment and conscience. On the day after the wedding he coolly informed his bride at the breakfast-table that they must part forever, giving for the pretext a reason so foul, so monstrous, that its repetition in these pages is impossible, from the shocking indecency of the atrocious subterfuge. Spite of tears and protestations, he deserted the bride of a day never to return to her nor communicate with her again. It is a matter of surprise that a man capable of such diabolical mendacity as Dr. Griswold has shown himself to be, should have found anything favorable to say in his memoir, nor would he have done so, probably, had not the poet's pre-eminent genius made the few truths to be found in the biography as familiar as household words to the literary world.

The next important statement made by Dr. Griswold, and unquestionably the most heinous falsehood to be found in the whole tissue of fabrication which has been so extensively copied as "The Life of Edgar A. Poe," is the statement in regard to Poe's alleged breaking of his engagement with Mrs. Sarah Helen Whitman, of Providence, Rhode Island. I may be permitted, in introducing what I have to offer on this subject, to present a letter elicited by Mr. Griswold's original statement, written by Mr. William J. Pabodie, an esteemed and influential citizen of Providence: —

TO THE EDITORS OF THE NEW YORK TRIBUNE:

In an article on American Literature in the "Westminster Review" for April, and in one on Edgar A. Poe in "Tait's Magazine" for the same month, we find a repetition of certain incorrect and injurious statements in regard to the deceased author, which should not longer be suffered to pass unnoticed. These statements have circulated through half-a-dozen foreign and domestic periodicals, and are presented with an ingenious variety of detail. As a specimen, we take a passage from Tait, who quotes as his authority Dr. Griswold's memoir of the poet: —

"Poe's life, in fact, during the three years that yet remained to him, was simply a repetition of his previous existence, notwithstanding which his reputation still increased, and he made many friends. He was, indeed, at one time, engaged to marry a lady who is termed 'one of the most brilliant women in New England.' He, however, suddenly changed his determination; and after declaring his intention to break the match, he crossed the same day into the city where the lady dwelt, and on the evening that should have been the evening before the bridal 'committed in drunkenness such outrages at her house as made necessary a summons of the police.'"

The subject is one which cannot well be approached without invading the sanctities of private life; and the *improbabilities* of the story may, to those acquainted with the parties, be deemed an all-sufficient refutation. But in view of the rapidly increasing circulation which this story has obtained, and the severity of comment which it has elicited, the friends of the late Edgar A. Poe deem it an imperative duty to free his memory from this unjust reproach, and to oppose to it their unqualified denial. Such a denial is due, not only to the memory of the departed, but also to the lady whose home is supposed to have been desecrated by these disgraceful outrages.

Mr. Poe was frequently my guest during his stay in Providence. In his several visits to the city I was with him daily. I was acquainted with the circumstances of his engagement and with the causes which led to its dissolution. I am authorized to say, not only from my personal knowledge, but also from the statements of *all* who were conversant with the affair, that there exists not a shadow of foundation for the stories above alluded to.

Mr. Poe's friends have no desire to palliate his faults, nor to conceal the fact of his intemperance, — a vice which, though never *habitual* to him, seems, according to Dr. Griswold's published statements, to have repeatedly assailed him at the most momentous epochs of his life. With the single exception of this fault, which he has so fearfully expiated, his conduct, during the period of my acquaintance with him, was invariably that of a man of honor and a gentleman; and I know that, in the hearts of all who knew him best among us, he is remembered with feelings of melancholy interest and generous sympathy.

We understand that Dr. Griswold has expressed his sincere regret that these unfounded reports should have been sanctioned by his authority; and we doubt not, if he possesses that fairness of character and uprightness of intention which we have ascribed to him, that he will do what lies in his power to remove an undeserved stigma from the memory of the departed.

WILLIAM J. PABODIE.

PROVIDENCE, June 2, 1852.

In answer to this, we find Dr. Griswold in the rôle of a bully, impudently attempting to put down Mr. Pabodie's dignified statement *vi et armis*. He writes to Mr. Pabodie a private letter as follows: —

NEW YORK, June 8, 1852.

*Dear Sir*, — I think you have done wrong in publishing your communication in yesterday's "Tribune" without ascertaining how it must be met. I have never expressed any such regrets as you write of, and I cannot permit any statement in my memoir of Poe to be contradicted by a reputable person, unless it is shown to be wrong. The statement in question I can easily prove on the most unquestionable authority to be true; and unless you explain your letter to the "Tribune" in another for publication there, you will compel me to place before the public such documents as will be infinitely painful to Mrs. Whitman and all others concerned. The person to whom he disclosed his intention to break off the match was Mrs. H——t. He was already engaged to another party. I am sorry for the publication of your letter. Why you did not permit me to see it before it appeared, and disclose in advance these consequences, I cannot conceive. I would willingly drop the subject, but for the controversies hitherto in regard to it, with which you are acquainted. Before writing to the "Tribune," I will await your opportunity to acknowledge this note, and to give such explanations of your letter as will render any public statement on my part unnecessary.

In haste, yours respectfully,

R. W. GRISWOLD.

W. J. PABODIE, Esq.

To this insolent and impotent letter, which was tesselated with scandalous and irrelevant stories respecting Mr. Poe's relations with some of his most esteemed and valued friends, Mr. Pabodie replied by calmly reiterating his published statement in the "New York Tribune," and by adducing further proof of Griswold's audacious fabrications. The tone of this letter is in striking contrast to that of Griswold's virulent and threatening note. Its forbearing mildness, indeed, renders it open to criticism on this ground: —

JUNE 11, 1852.

Mr. RUFUS W. GRISWOLD:

*Dear Sir,* — In reply to your note, I would say that I have simply testified to what *I know to be true*, namely, that no such incident as that so extensively circulated in regard to certain alleged outrages at the house of Mrs. Whitman, and the calling of the police, ever took place. The assertion that Mr. Poe came to Providence the last time with the intention of breaking off the engagement you will find equally unfounded, when I have stated to you the facts as I know them. In remarking that you had expressed regret at the fact of their admission into your memoir, I had reference to a passage in a letter written by Mrs. H. to Mrs. W., which was read to me by the latter some time since. I stated in all truthfulness the impression which that letter had left upon my mind. I enclose an extract from the letter, that you may judge for yourself: —

> "Having heard that Mr. Poe was engaged to a lady of Providence, I said to him, on hearing that he was going to that city, 'Mr. Poe, are you going to Providence to be married?'—'I am going to deliver a lecture on Poetry,' he replied. Then, after a pause, and with a look of great reserve, he added, 'That marriage may never take place.'" *

I know that from the commencement of Poe's acquaintance with Mrs. W., he *repeatedly urged her to an immediate marriage.* At the time of his interview with Mrs. H., circumstances existed which threatened to postpone the marriage indefinitely, if not altogether to prevent it. It was, undoubtedly, with reference to these circumstances that his remark to Mrs. H. was made, certainly not to breaking off the engagement, as his subsequent conduct will prove. He left New York for Providence on the afternoon of his interview with Mrs. H., not with any view to the proposed union, but at the solicitation of the Providence Lyceum; and on the evening of his arrival delivered his lecture on American Poetry, before an audience of some two thousand persons. During his stay he again succeeded in renewing his engagement and in obtaining Mrs. W.'s consent to an immediate marriage.

* In another letter Mrs. H. writes, referring to this conversation, indignant at the use which Dr. Griswold had made of these innocent words more than a year after she had reported them, "These were Mr. Poe's words, and these were all."

He stopped at the Earl House, where he became acquainted with a set of somewhat dissolute young men, who often invited him to drink with them. We all know that he sometimes yielded to such temptations, and on the third or fourth evening after his lecture, he came up to Mrs. Whitman's in a state of partial intoxication. I was myself present nearly the whole evening, and do most solemnly affirm that there was no noise, no disturbance, no "outrage," neither was there any "call for the police." Mr. Poe said but little. This was undoubtedly the evening referred to in your memoir, for it was the *only* evening in which he was intoxicated during his last visit to this city; but it was not "the evening that should have been before the bridal," for they were not then published, and the law in our State required that they should be published at least three times, on as many different occasions, before they could be legally married.

The next morning, Mr. Poe manifested and expressed the most profound contrition and regret, and was profuse in his promises of amendment. He was still urgently anxious that the marriage should take place before he left the city.

That very morning he wrote a note to Dr. Crocker, requesting him to publish the intended marriage at the earliest opportunity, and intrusted this note to me, with the request that I should deliver it in person. You will perceive, therefore, that I did not write unadvisedly in the statement published in the "Tribune."

For yourself, Mr. Griswold, I entertain none other than the kindest feelings. I was not surprised that you should have believed those rumors in regard to Poe and his engagement; and although, from a regard for the feelings of the lady, I do not think that a belief in their truth could possibly justify their publication, yet I was not disposed to impute to you any wrong motive in presenting them to the public. I supposed rather that, in the hurry of publication and in the multiplicity of your avocations, you had not given each statement that precise consideration which less haste and more leisure would have permitted. I was thus easily led to believe, from Mrs. H.'s letter, that upon being assured of their incorrectness, and upon learning how exceedingly painful they were to the feelings of the surviving party, you sincerely regretted their publication. I would fain hope so still.

In my article in the "Tribune," I endeavored to palliate their publication on your part, and to say everything in your extenuation that was consistent with the demands of truth and justice to the parties concerned. I would add, in regard to Poe's intoxication on the evening above alluded to, that to all appearances it was as purely accidental and unpremeditated as any similar act of his life. By what species of logic, any one should infer that, in this particular instance, it was the result of a malicious purpose and deliberate design, I have never been able to conceive. The facts of the case, and his subsequent conduct, prove beyond a doubt that he had no such design.

With great respect,

Your obedient servant,

WILLIAM J. PABODIE.

REV. RUFUS W. GRISWOLD.

It will be seen by this correspondence that the attempt of Dr. Griswold to browbeat Mr. Pabodie was courteously but firmly and unanswerably met. Dr. Griswold never paid the slightest attention to this letter, contenting himself with leaving on record the outrageous scandal that has since obtained an almost unprecedented circulation in the numerous memoirs of Poe, based upon Dr. Griswold's malicious invention, that have been published. The introduction of the story of the banns would seem to come under the head of what lawyers call "an accessory after the fact." Dr. Griswold had probably heard that the banns were *written*, if not *published*, and took advantage of this information to adroitly garnish his story with them. To set this question at rest forever, I have obtained permission to quote the following passages of a letter received from Mrs. Whitman in August, 1873: —

"No such scene as that described by Dr. Griswold ever transpired in my presence. No one, certainly no woman, who had the slightest acquaintance with Edgar Poe could have credited the story for an instant. He was *essentially* and *instinctively* a gentleman, utterly incapable, even in moments of excitement and delirium, of such an outrage as Dr. Griswold has ascribed to him. No authentic anecdote of coarse indulgence in vulgar orgies or bestial riot has ever been recorded of him. During the last years of his unhappy life, whenever he yielded to the temptation that was drawing him into its fathomless abyss, as with the resistless swirl of the maelstrom, he always lost himself in sublime rhapsodies on the evolution of the universe, speaking as from some imaginary platform to vast audiences of rapt and attentive listeners. During one of his visits to this city, in the autumn of 1848, I once saw him, after one of those nights of wild excitement, before reason had fully recovered its throne. Yet even *then*, in those frenzied moments when the doors of the mind's 'Haunted Palace' were left all unguarded, his words were the words of a princely intellect, overwrought, and of a heart only too sensitive and too finely strung. I repeat that no one acquainted with Edgar Poe could have given Dr. Griswold's scandalous anecdote a moment's credence.

"Yours, etc.,

"S. H. WHITMAN."

In regard to Mr. Griswold's professed friendship for Poe, which he endeavors to demonstrate in copies of a correspondence which I cannot refrain from thinking was extensively "doctored" by the doctor, to suit his purpose, I am able to present an extract from an autograph letter of Dr. Griswold written to Mrs. Whitman in 1849.

The object of this was evidently to cool Mrs. Whitman's friendship for Mrs. Clemm, thus preventing their further intimacy. This was desirable to Dr. Griswold for evident reasons.

NEW YORK, December 17, 1849.

MY DEAR MRS. WHITMAN:

I have been two or three weeks in Philadelphia attending to the remains which a recent fire left of my library and furniture, and so did not receive your interesting letter in regard to our departed acquaintance until to-day. I wrote, as you suppose, the notice of Poe in the "Tribune," but very hastily.

I was not his friend, nor was he mine, as I remember to have told you. I undertook to edit his writings to oblige Mrs. Clemm, and they will soon be published in two thick volumes, of which a copy shall be sent to you. I saw very little of Poe in his last years. . . . I cannot refrain from begging you to be *very* careful what you say or write to Mrs. Clemm, who is not your friend, nor anybody's friend, and who has no element of goodness or kindness in her nature, but whose whole heart and understanding are full of malice and wickedness. *I confide in you* these sentences for your own sake only, for Mrs. C. appears to be *a very warm friend to me.* Pray destroy this note, and, at least, act cautiously, till I may justify it in a conversation with you.

I am yours very sincerely,

RUFUS W. GRISWOLD.

This brief note affords a tolerably good specimen of the utter duplicity of the man. In his printed memoir of Poe, he quotes a correspondence indicating professed friendship; in private, he squarely owns that no friendship ever existed between Poe and himself.

He writes that Mrs. Clemm is a friend to no one, and stigmatizes her character, and in the same breath speaks of her warm friendship for him.

Had Griswold lived in Othello's time, no one could have disputed with him the position of "mine ancient," honest Iago.

From a correspondence from Mrs. Clemm, who, there can be no reasonable doubt, is correctly described by Willis as "one of those angels upon earth that women in adversity can be," we find the most positive testimony that Dr. Griswold's association with collecting the works of Poe, and of writing a memoir of the author, was purely voluntary and speculative.

It presents simply the fact of a designing and unscrupulous man, prompted by hatred and greed of gain, taking advantage of a helpless woman, unaccustomed to business, to defraud her of her rights, and gratify his malice and his avarice at her expense.

A miserable pittance having been given to Mrs. Clemm in exchange for Poe's private papers, Dr. Griswold draws up a paper for Mrs. Clemm to sign, announcing his appointment as Poe's literary executor, not omitting of course a touching allusion to himself. This is duly signed by Mrs. Clemm, and printed over her signature in the published editions of Poe's works. But if the wording of this curious paper be carefully observed, it will be noted that nothing whatever is said in it of any request by Poe that Dr. Griswold should write a memoir of his life. This duty was properly assigned to Mr. Willis, — of all men familiar with the subject the most competent to fulfil such a task, — and his tender and manly tribute to the stricken genius was all that could have been wished, all that the world called for.

Mrs. Clemm had no idea, at the time she signed the paper which she scarcely understood, that Dr. Griswold had any intention of supplementing Mr. Willis's obituary with any memoir by his own pen. It was a piece of gratuitous malice, — the act of a fiend exulting over a dead and helpless victim.

The tone of Poe's critique of Griswold, in his review of the "Poets and Poetry of America," which unquestionably inspired the reverend doctor's malignant hatred, scathing as it is, will impress the reader with its outspoken manliness and integrity of purpose. What a contrast to the biography that, while undermining the very foundations of Poe's moral and social character, yet hypocritically professes to be dictated by friendship, and written in a *generous* spirit! I fear that Dr. Griswold's precious specimen of his generosity will go on record in the history of literature as an everlasting monument of his despicable meanness.

Dr. Griswold was, take him all in all, about as well fitted to be Poe's biographer, as Mr. Preston Brooks would have been to have written an impartial life of Charles Sumner. And, indeed, whenever it becomes possible for a Rufus W. Griswold to write a true transcript of the life of an Edgar A. Poe, then will perpetual motion have become possible, the world will find it easy and comfortable to arrest its revolutions at pleasure, and balloon voyages to the planets will become as popular and as practicable as is a trip to Saratoga at the present day.

## THE RAVEN.

ONCE upon a midnight dreary, while I pondered, weak and weary,
Over many a quaint and curious volume of forgotten lore —
While I nodded, nearly napping, suddenly there came a tapping,
As of some one gently rapping, rapping at my chamber door.
"'T is some visitor," I muttered, "tapping at my chamber door —
Only this and nothing more."

Ah, distinctly I remember it was in the bleak December,
And each separate dying ember wrought its ghost upon the floor.
Eagerly I wished the morrow; — vainly I had sought to borrow
From my books surcease of sorrow — sorrow for the lost Lenore —
For the rare and radiant maiden whom the angels name Lenore —
Nameless here for evermore.

And the silken sad uncertain rustling of each purple curtain
Thrilled me — filled me with fantastic terrors never felt before;
So that now, to still the beating of my heart, I stood repeating
"'T is some visitor entreating entrance at my chamber door —
Some late visitor entreating entrance at my chamber door;
This it is and nothing more."

Presently my soul grew stronger; hesitating then no longer,
"Sir," said I, "or Madam, truly your forgiveness I implore;
But the fact is I was napping, and so gently you came rapping,
And so faintly you came tapping, tapping at my chamber door,
That I scarce was sure I heard you" — here I opened wide the door; —
Darkness there and nothing more.

Deep into that darkness peering, long I stood there wondering, fearing,
Doubting, dreaming dreams no mortals ever dared to dream before;

But the silence was unbroken, and the stillness gave no
token,
And the only word there spoken was the whispered
word, "Lenore?"
This I whispered, and an echo murmured back the word,
"Lenore!"
Merely this and nothing more.

Back into the chamber turning, all my soul within me
burning,
Soon again I heard a tapping, something louder than
before.
"Surely," said I, "surely that is something at my window lattice;
Let me see, then, what thereat is and this mystery
explore —
Let my heart be still a moment and this mystery explore; —
'T is the wind and nothing more."

Open here I flung the shutter, when, with many a flirt
and flutter,
In there stepped a stately Raven of the saintly days of
yore.
Not the least obeisance made he; not a minute stopped
or stayed he,
But, with mien of lord or lady, perched above my chamber door —

Perched upon a bust of Pallas just above my chamber door —
Perched, and sat, and nothing more.

Then this ebony bird beguiling my sad fancy into smiling,
By the grave and stern decorum of the countenance it wore,
"Though thy crest be shorn and shaven, thou," I said, "art sure no craven,
Ghastly, grim, and ancient Raven, wandering from the Nightly shore.
Tell me what thy lordly name is on the Night's Plutonian shore!"
Quoth the Raven, "Nevermore."

Much I marvelled this ungainly fowl to hear discourse so plainly,
Though its answer little meaning — little relevancy bore;
For we cannot help agreeing that no living human being
Ever yet was blessed with seeing bird above his chamber door —
Bird or beast upon the sculptured bust above his chamber door,
With such name as "Nevermore."

But the Raven, sitting lonely on that placid bust, spoke only
That one word, as if his soul in that one word he did outpour.

Nothing further then he uttered; not a feather then he
fluttered —
Till I scarcely more than muttered, "Other friends have
flown before —
On the morrow *he* will leave me, as my Hopes have
flown before,"
Then the bird said "Nevermore."

Startled at the stillness broken by reply so aptly spoken,
"Doubtless," said I, "what it utters is its only stock
and store
Caught from some unhappy master whom unmerciful
Disaster
Followed fast and followed faster till his songs one bur-
den bore —
Till the dirges of his Hope that melancholy burden bore
Of 'Never, — nevermore.'"

But the Raven still beguiling all my sad soul into smiling,
Straight I wheeled a cushioned seat in front of bird and
bust and door;
Then, upon the velvet sinking, I betook myself to linking
Fancy unto fancy, thinking what this ominous bird of
yore —
What this grim, ungainly, ghastly, gaunt, and ominous
bird of yore
Meant in croaking "Nevermore."

This I sat engaged in guessing, but no syllable expressing
To the fowl whose fiery eyes now burned into my bosom's core;
This and more I sat divining, with my head at ease reclining
On the cushion's velvet lining that the lamplight gloated o'er,
But whose velvet violet lining with the lamplight gloating o'er
*She* shall press, ah, nevermore!

Then, methought, the air grew denser, perfumed from an unseen censer
Swung by Seraphim whose footfalls tinkled on the tufted floor.
"Wretch," I cried, "thy God hath lent thee — by these angels he hath sent thee
Respite — respite and nepenthe from thy memories of Lenore!
Quaff, oh quaff this kind Nepenthe and forget this lost Lenore!"
Quoth the Raven, "Nevermore."

"Prophet!" said I, "thing of evil! — prophet still, if bird or devil!
Whether Tempter sent, or whether tempest tossed thee here ashore,

Desolate yet all undaunted, on this desert land enchanted —
On this Home by horror haunted — tell me truly, I implore —
Is there — *is* there balm in Gilead? — tell me — tell me, I implore!"
Quoth the Raven, "Nevermore."

"Prophet!" said I, "thing of evil — prophet still, if bird or devil!
By that Heaven that bends above us — by that God we both adore —
Tell this soul with sorrow laden if, within the distant Aidenn,
It shall clasp a sainted maiden whom the angels name Lenore —
Clasp a rare and radiant maiden whom the angels name Lenore."
Quoth the Raven, "Nevermore."

"Be that word our sign of parting, bird or fiend!" I shrieked, upstarting —
"Get thee back into the tempest and the Night's Plutonian shore!
Leave no black plume as a token of that lie thy soul hath spoken!
Leave my loneliness unbroken! — quit the bust above my door!

Take thy beak from out my heart, and take thy form
from off my door!"
Quoth the Raven, "Nevermore."

And the Raven, never flitting, still is sitting, still is
sitting
On the pallid bust of Pallas just above my chamber
door;
And his eyes have all the seeming of a demon's that is
dreaming,
And the lamplight o'er him streaming throws his shadow
on the floor;
And my soul from out that shadow that lies floating on
the floor
Shall be lifted — nevermore!

---

## LENORE.

AH, broken is the golden bowl! the spirit flown
forever!
Let the bell toll! — a saintly soul floats on the
Stygian river;
And, Guy De Vere, hast *thou* no tear? — weep now or
nevermore!

See! on yon drear and rigid bier low lies thy love,
Lenore!

Come! let the burial rite be read — the funeral song be sung! —
An anthem for the queenliest dead that ever died so young —
A dirge for her the doubly dead in that she died so young.

"Wretches! ye loved her for her wealth and hated her for her pride;
And when she fell in feeble health, ye blessed her — that she died!
How *shall* the ritual, then, be read? — the requiem how be sung
By you — by yours, the evil eye, — by yours, the slanderous tongue
That did to death the innocence that died, and died so young?"
*Peccavimus;* but rave not thus! and let a Sabbath song
Go up to God so solemnly the dead may feel no wrong!
The sweet Lenore hath "gone before," with Hope, that flew beside,
Leaving thee wild for the dear child that should have been thy bride —
For her, the fair and *debonair,* that now so lowly lies,
The life upon her yellow hair but not within her eyes —
The life still there, upon her hair — the death upon her eyes.

"Avaunt! to-night my heart is light. No dirge will I upraise,
But waft the angel on her flight with a Pæan of old days!
Let *no* bell toll! — lest her sweet soul, amid its hallowed mirth,
Should catch the note, as it doth float up from the damnèd Earth.
To friends above, from fiends below, the indignant ghost is riven —
From Hell unto a high estate far up within the Heaven —
From grief and groan, to a golden throne, beside the King of Heaven."

---

## HYMN.

T morn — at noon — at twilight dim —
Maria! thou hast heard my hymn!
In joy and woe — in good and ill —
Mother of God, be with me still!
When the Hours flew brightly by,
And not a cloud obscured the sky,
My soul, lest it should truant be,
Thy grace did guide to thine and thee;
Now, when storms of Fate o'ercast
Darkly my Present and my Past,
Let my Future radiant shine
With sweet hopes of thee and thine!

## A VALENTINE.

FOR her this rhyme is penned, whose luminous eyes,
Brightly expressive as the twins of Lœda,
Shall find her own sweet name, that, nestling lies
Upon the page, enwrapped from every reader.
Search narrowly the lines! — they hold a treasure
Divine — a talisman — an amulet
That must be worn *at heart.* Search well the measure —
The words — the syllables! Do not forget
The trivialest point, or you may lose your labor!
And yet there is in this no Gordian knot
Which one might not undo without a sabre,
If one could merely comprehend the plot.
Enwritten upon the leaf where now are peering
Eyes scintillating soul, there lie *perdus*
Three eloquent words oft uttered in the hearing
Of poets, by poets — as the name is a poet's, too.
Its letters, although naturally lying
Like the knight Pinto — Mendez Ferdinando —
Still form a synonym for Truth. — Cease trying!
You will not read the riddle, though you do the best
you *can* do.

[*To translate the address, read the first letter of the first line in connection with the second letter of the second line, the third letter of the third line, the fourth of the fourth, and so on to the end. The name will thus appear.*]

## THE COLISEUM.

TYPE of the antique Rome! Rich reliquary
Of lofty contemplation left to Time
By buried centuries of pomp and power!
At length — at length — after so many days
Of weary pilgrimage and burning thirst,
(Thirst for the springs of lore that in thee lie,)
I kneel, an altered and an humble man,
Amid thy shadows, and so drink within
My very soul thy grandeur, gloom, and glory!

Vastness! and Age! and Memories of Eld!
Silence! and Desolation! and dim Night!
I feel ye now — I feel ye in your strength —
O spells more sure than e'er Judæan king
Taught in the gardens of Gethsemane!
O charms more potent than the rapt Chaldee
Ever drew down from out the quiet stars!

Here, where a hero fell, a column falls!
Here, where the mimic eagle glared in gold,
A midnight vigil holds the swarthy bat!
Here, where the dames of Rome their gilded hair
Waved to the wind, now wave the reed and thistle!
Here, where on golden throne the monarch lolled,
Glides, spectre-like, unto his marble home,
Lit by the wan light of the hornéd moon,
The swift and silent lizard of the stones!

But stay! these walls — these ivy-clad arcades —
These mouldering plinths — these sad and blackened shafts —
These vague entablatures — this crumbling frieze —
These shattered cornices — this wreck — this ruin —
These stones — alas! these gray stones — are they all —
All of the famed, and the colossal left
By the corrosive Hours to Fate and me?

"Not all" — the Echoes answer me — "not all!
Prophetic sounds and loud, arise forever
From us, and from all Ruin, unto the wise,
As melody from Memnon to the Sun.
We rule the hearts of mightiest men — we rule
With a despotic sway all giant minds.
We are not impotent — we pallid stones.
Not all our power is gone — not all our fame —
Not all the magic of our high renown —
Not all the wonder that encircles us —
Not all the mysteries that in us lie —
Not all the memories that hang upon
And cling around about us as a garment,
Clothing us in a robe of more than glory."

## TO HELEN.

I SAW thee once — once only — years ago:
I must not say *how* many — but *not* many.
It was a July midnight; and from out
A full-orbed moon, that, like thine own soul, soaring,
Sought a precipitate pathway up through heaven,
There fell a silvery silken veil of light,
With quietude, and sultriness, and slumber,
Upon the upturn'd faces of a thousand
Roses that grew in an enchanted garden,
Where no wind dared to stir, unless on tiptoe —
Fell on the upturn'd faces of these roses
That gave out, in return for the love-light,
Their odorous souls in an ecstatic death —
Fell on the upturn'd faces of these roses
That smiled and died in this parterre, enchanted
By thee, and by the poetry of thy presence.

Clad all in white, upon a violet bank
I saw thee half reclining; while the moon
Fell on the upturn'd faces of the roses,
And on thine own, upturn'd — alas, in sorrow!

Was it not Fate, that, on this July midnight —
Was it not Fate (whose name is also Sorrow)
That bade me pause before that garden-gate,
To breathe the incense of those slumbering roses?
No footstep stirred: the hated world all slept,
Save only thee and me. (Oh, Heaven! — oh, God!

How my heart beats in coupling those two words !)
Save only thee and me. I paused — I looked —
And in an instant all things disappeared.
(Ah, bear in mind this garden was enchanted !)

The pearly lustre of the moon went out:
The mossy banks and the meandering paths,
The happy flowers and the repining trees,
Were seen no more: the very roses' odors
Died in the arms of the adoring airs.
All — all expired save thee — save less than thou:
Save only the divine light in thine eyes —
Save but the soul in thine uplifted eyes.
I saw but them — they were the world to me.
I saw but them — saw only them for hours —
Saw only them until the moon went down.
What wild heart-histories seemed to lie enwritten
Upon those crystalline, celestial spheres !
How dark a woe ! yet how sublime a hope !
How silently serene a sea of pride !
How daring an ambition ! yet how deep —
How fathomless a capacity for love !

But now, at length, dear Dian sank from sight,
Into a western couch of thunder-cloud;
And thou, a ghost, amid the entombing trees
Didst glide way. *Only thine eyes remained.*
They *would not* go — they never yet have gone.

Lighting my lonely pathway home that night,
*They* have not left me (as my hopes have) since.
They follow me — they lead me through the years —
They are my ministers — yet I their slave.
Their office is to illumine and enkindle —
My duty, *to be saved* by their bright light,
And purified in their electric fire,
And sanctified in their elysian fire.
They fill my soul with Beauty (which is Hope),
And are far up in Heaven — the stars I kneel to
In the sad, silent watches of my night;
While even in the meridian glare of day
I see them still — two sweetly scintillant
Venuses, unextinguished by the sun!

---

## TO —— ——.

NOT long ago, the writer of these lines,
In the mad pride of intellectuality,
Maintained "the power of words" — denied [that ever
A thought arose within the human brain
Beyond the utterance of the human tongue:
And now, as if in mockery of that boast,
Two words — two foreign soft dissyllables —
Italian tones, made only to be murmured
By angels dreaming in the moonlit "dew
That hangs like chains of pearl on Hermon hill," —

Have stirred from out the abysses of his heart,
Unthought-like thoughts that are the souls of thought,
Richer, far wilder, far diviner visions
Than even the seraph harper, Israfel,
(Who has "the sweetest voice of all God's creatures,")
Could hope to utter. And I! my spells are broken.
The pen falls powerless from my shivering hand.
With thy dear name as text, though bidden by thee,
I cannot write — I cannot speak or think —
Alas, I cannot feel; for 't is not feeling,
This standing motionless upon the golden
Threshold of the wide-open gate of dreams,
Gazing, entranced, adown the gorgeous vista,
And thrilling as I see, upon the right,
Upon the left, and all the way along,
Amid unpurpled vapors, far away
To where the prospect terminates — *thee only.*

---

## ULALUME.

THE skies they were ashen and sober;
The leaves they were crispèd and sere —
The leaves they were withering and sere —
It was night in the lonesome October
Of my most immemorial year;

It was hard by the dim lake of Auber,
    In the misty mid region of Weir —
It was down by the dank tarn of Auber,
    In the ghoul-haunted woodland of Weir.

Here once, through an alley Titanic,
    Of cypress, I roamed with my soul —
    Of cypress, with Psyche, my Soul.
These were days when my heart was volcanic
    As the scoriac rivers that roll —
    As the lavas that restlessly roll —
Their sulphurous currents down Yaanek
    In the ultimate climes of the pole —
That groan as they roll down Mount Yaanek
    In the realms of the boreal pole.

Our talk had been serious and sober,
    But our thoughts they were palsied and sere —
    Our memories were treacherous and sere —
For we knew not the month was October,
    And we marked not the night of the year —
    (Ah, night of all nights in the year!)
We noted not the dim lake of Auber —
    (Though once we had journeyed down here) —
Remembered not the dank tarn of Auber,
    Nor the ghoul-haunted woodland of Weir.

And now, as the night was senescent
    And star-dials pointed to morn —
    As the star-dials hinted of morn —
At the end of our path a liquescent
    And nebulous lustre was born,
Out of which a miraculous crescent
    Arose with a duplicate horn —
Astarte's bediamonded crescent
    Distinct with its duplicate horn.

And I said — "She is warmer than Dian:
    She rolls through an ether of sighs —
    She revels in a region of sighs:
She has seen that the tears are not dry on
    These cheeks, where the worm never dies,
And has come past the stars of the Lion
    To point us the path to the skies —
    To the Lethean peace of the skies —
Come up, in despite of the Lion,
    To shine on us with her bright eyes —
Come up through the lair of the Lion,
    With love in her luminous eyes."

But Psyche, uplifting her finger,
    Said — "Sadly this star I mistrust —
    Her pallor I strangely mistrust: —
Oh, hasten! oh, let us not linger!
    Oh, fly! — let us fly! — for we must."

In terror she spoke, letting sink her
    Wings until they trailed in the dust —
In agony sobbed, letting sink her
    Plumes till they trailed in the dust —
    Till they sorrowfully trailed in the dust.

I replied — "This is nothing but dreaming:
    Let us on by this tremulous light!
    Let us bathe in this crystalline light!
Its Sybilic splendor is beaming
    With Hope and in Beauty to-night: —
    See! — it flickers up the sky through the night!
Ah, we safely may trust to its gleaming,
    And be sure it will lead us aright —
We safely may trust to a gleaming
    That cannot but guide us aright,
    Since it flickers up to Heaven through the night."

Thus I pacified Psyche and kissed her,
    And tempted her out of her gloom —
    And conquered her scruples and gloom;
And we passed to the end of the vista,
    But were stopped by the door of a tomb —
    By the door of a legended tomb;
And I said — "What is written, sweet sister,
    On the door of this legended tomb?"
    She replied — "Ulalume — Ulalume —
    'T is the vault of thy lost Ulalume!"

Then my heart it grew ashen and sober
    As the leaves that were crisped and sere —
    As the leaves that were withering and sere,
And I cried — " It was surely October
    On *this* very night of last year
    That I journeyed — I journeyed down here —
    That I brought a dread burden down here —
    On this night of all nights in the year,
    Ah, what demon has tempted me here?
Well I know, now, this dim lake of Auber —
    This misty mid region of Weir —
Well I know, now, this dank tarn of Auber,
    This ghoul-haunted woodland of Weir."

---

## THE BELLS.

I.

HEAR the sledges with the bells —
    Silver bells!
What a world of merriment their melody foretells!
    How they tinkle, tinkle, tinkle,
        In the icy air of night!
    While the stars that oversprinkle
    All the heavens, seem to twinkle
        With a crystalline delight;
      Keeping time, time, time,
      In a sort of Runic rhyme,

To the tintinabulation that so musically wells
From the bells, bells, bells, bells,
Bells, bells, bells —
From the jingling and the tinkling of the bells.

II.

Hear the mellow wedding bells,
Golden bells!
What a world of happiness their harmony foretells!
Through the balmy air of night
How they ring out their delight!
From the molten golden notes,
And all in tune,
What a liquid ditty floats
To the turtle-dove that listens, while she gloats
On the moon!
Oh, from out the sounding cells,
What a gush of euphony voluminously wells!
How it swells!
How it dwells
On the Future! how it tells
Of the rapture that impels
To the swinging and the ringing
Of the bells, bells, bells,
Of the bells, bells, bells, bells,
Bells, bells, bells —
To the rhyming and the chiming of the bells!

III.

Hear the loud alarum bells —
Brazen bells !
What a tale of terror, now, their turbulency tells !
In the startled ear of night
How they scream out their affright !
Too much horrified to speak,
They can only shriek, shriek,
Out of tune,
In a clamorous appealing to the mercy of the fire,
In a mad expostulation with the deaf and frantic fire.
Leaping higher, higher, higher,
With a desperate desire,
And a resolute endeavor
Now — now to sit or never,
By the side of the pale-faced moon.
Oh, the bells, bells, bells !
What a tale their terror tells
Of Despair !
How they clang, and clash, and roar !
What a horror they outpour
On the bosom of the palpitating air !
Yet the ear it fully knows,
By the twanging,
And the clanging,
How the danger ebbs and flows ;

Yet the ear distinctly tells,
In the jangling,
And the wrangling,
How the danger sinks and swells,
By the sinking or the swelling in the anger of the bells —
Of the bells —
Of the bells, bells, bells, bells,
Bells, bells, bells —
In the clamor and the clangor of the bells!

IV.

Hear the tolling of the bells —
Iron bells!
What a world of solemn thought their monody compels!
In the silence of the night,
How we shiver with affright
At the melancholy menace of their tone!
For every sound that floats
From the rust within their throats
Is a groan.
And the people — ah, the people —
They that dwell up in the steeple,
All alone,
And who tolling, tolling, tolling,
In that muffled monotone,
Feel a glory in so rolling
On the human heart a stone —

They are neither man nor woman —
They are neither brute nor human —
They are Ghouls:
And their king it is who tolls;
And he rolls, rolls, rolls,
Rolls
A pæan from the bells!
And his merry bosom swells
With the pæan of the bells!
And he dances, and he yells;
Keeping time, time, time,
In a sort of Runic rhyme,
To the pæan of the bells —
Of the bells:
Keeping time, time, time,
In a sort of Runic rhyme,
To the throbbing of the bells —
Of the bells, bells, bells —
To the sobbing of the bells;
Keeping time, time, time,
As he knells, knells, knells,
In a happy Runic rhyme,
To the rolling of the bells —
Of the bells, bells, bells —
To the tolling of the bells,
Of the bells, bells, bells, bells —
Bells, bells, bells —
To the moaning and the groaning of the bells.

## AN ENIGMA.

"SELDOM we find," says Solomon Don Dunce,
"Half an idea in the profoundest sonnet.
Through all the flimsy things we see at once
As easily as through a Naples bonnet—
Trash of all trash!—how *can* a lady don it!
Yet heavier far than your Petrarchan stuff—
Owl-downy nonsense that the faintest puff
Twirls into trunk-paper the while you con it."
And, veritably, Sol is right enough.
The general tuckermanities are arrant
Bubbles—ephemeral and *so* transparent—
But *this* is, now,—you may depend upon it—
Stable, opaque, immortal—all by dint
Of the dear names that lie concealed within 't.

---

## ANNABEL LEE.

IT was many and many a year ago,
In a kingdom by the sea,
That a maiden there lived whom you may know
By the name of ANNABEL LEE;
And this maiden she lived with no other thought
Than to love and be loved by me.

*I* was a child and *she* was a child,
    In this kingdom by the sea:
But we loved with a love that was more than love —
    I and my ANNABEL LEE;
With a love that the winged seraphs of heaven
    Coveted her and me.

And this was the reason that, long ago,
    In this kingdom by the sea,
A wind blew out of a cloud, chilling
    My beautiful ANNABEL LEE;
So that her high-born kinsman came
    And bore her away from me,
To shut her up in a sepulchre
    In this kingdom by the sea.

The angels, not half so happy in heaven,
    Went envying her and me —
Yes! — that was the reason (as all men know,
    In this kingdom by the sea)
That the wind came out of the cloud by night,
    Chilling and killing my ANNABEL LEE.

But our love it was stronger by far than the love
    Of those who were older than we —
    Of many far wiser than we —
And neither the angels in heaven above,
    Nor the demons down under the sea,
Can ever dissever my soul from the soul
    Of the beautiful ANNABEL LEE:

For the moon never beams, without bringing me dreams
Of the beautiful ANNABEL LEE;
And the stars never rise, but I feel the bright eyes
Of the beautiful ANNABEL LEE;
And so, all the night-tide, I lie down by the side
Of my darling — my darling — my life and my bride,
In the sepulchre there by the sea,
In her tomb by the sounding sea.

---

## TO MY MOTHER.

BECAUSE I feel that, in the Heavens above,
The angels, whispering to one another,
Can find, among their burning terms of love,
None so devotional as that of "Mother,"
Therefore by that dear name I long have called you —
You who are more than mother unto me,
And fill my heart of hearts, where Death installed you,
In setting my Virginia's spirit free.
My mother — my own mother, who died early,
Was but the mother of myself; but you
Are mother to the one I loved so dearly,
And thus are dearer than the mother I knew
By that infinity with which my wife
Was dearer to my soul than its own soul-life.

## THE HAUNTED PALACE.

IN the greenest of our valleys
By good angels tenanted,
Once a fair and stately palace —
Radiant palace — reared its head.
In the monarch Thought's dominion —
It stood there !
Never seraph spread a pinion
Over fabric half so fair !

Banners yellow, glorious, golden,
On its roof did float and flow,
(This — all this — was in the olden
Time long ago,)
And every gentle air that dallied,
In that sweet day,
Along the ramparts plumed and pallid,
A wingèd odor went away.

Wanderers in that happy valley,
Through two luminous windows, saw
Spirits moving musically,
To a lute's well-tunèd law,
Round about a throne where, sitting
(Porphyrogene !)
In state his glory well befitting,
The ruler of the realm was seen.

And all with pearl and ruby glowing
  Was the fair palace door,
Through which came flowing, flowing, flowing
  And sparkling evermore,
A troop of Echoes, whose sweet duty
  Was but to sing,
In voices of surpassing beauty,
  The wit and wisdom of their king.

But evil things, in robes of sorrow,
  Assailed the monarch's high estate.
(Ah, let us mourn! — for never morrow
  Shall dawn upon him desolate!)
And round about his home the glory
  That blushed and bloomed,
Is but a dim-remembered story
  Of the old time entombed.

And travellers, now, within that valley,
  Through the red-litten windows see
Vast forms, that move fantastically
  To a discordant melody,
While, like a ghastly rapid river,
  Through the pale door
A hideous throng rush out forever
  And laugh — but smile no more.

## THE CONQUERER WORM.

LO! 't is a gala night
  Within the lonesome latter years.
An angel throng, bewinged, bedight
  In veils, and drowned in tears,
Sit in a theatre, to see
  A play of hopes and fears,
While the orchestra breathes fitfully
  The music of the spheres.

Mimes, in the form of God on high,
  Mutter and mumble low,
And hither and thither fly —
  Mere puppets they, who come and go
At bidding of vast formless things
  That shift the scenery to and fro,
Flapping from out their Condor wings
  Invisible Woe!

That motley drama — oh, be sure
  It shall not be forgot!
With its Phantom chased for evermore,
  By a crowd that seize it not,
Through a circle that ever returneth in
  To the self-same spot,
And much of Madness, and more of Sin,
  And Horror the soul of the plot.

But see, amid the mimic rout
  A crawling shape intrude!
A blood-red thing that writhes from out
  The scenic solitude!
It writhes! — it writhes! — with mortal pangs
  The mimes become its food,
And the angels sob at vermin fangs
  In human gore imbrued.

Out — out are the lights — out all!
  And, over each quivering form,
The curtain, a funeral pall,
  Comes down with the rush of a storm,
And the angels, all pallid and wan,
  Uprising, unveiling, affirm
That the play is the tragedy, "Man,"
  And its hero the Conqueror Worm.

---

## TO F——S S. O——D.

THOU wouldst be loved? — then let thy heart
  From its present pathway part not!
Being everything which now thou art,
  Be nothing which thou art not.
So with the world thy gentle ways,
  Thy grace, thy more than beauty,
Shall be an endless theme of praise,
  And love — a simple duty.

## TO ONE IN PARADISE.

THOU wast that all to me, love,
For which my soul did pine —
A green isle in the sea, love,
A fountain and a shrine,
All wreathed with fairy fruits and flowers,
And all the flowers were mine.

Ah, dream too bright to last!
Ah, starry Hope! that didst arise
But to be overcast!
A voice from out the Future cries,
"On! on!" — but o'er the Past
(Dim gulf!) my spirit hovering lies
Mute, motionless, aghast!

For, alas! alas! with me
The light of Life is o'er!
"No more — no more — no more —"
(Such language holds the solemn sea
To the sands upon the shore)
Shall bloom the thunder-blasted tree,
Or the stricken eagle soar!

And all my days are trances,
And all my nightly dreams
Are where thy dark eye glances,
And where thy footstep gleams —
In what ethereal dances,
By what eternal streams.

## THE VALLEY OF UNREST.

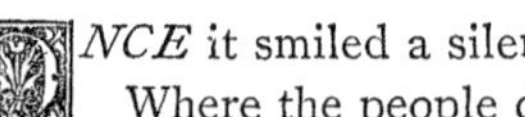

*NCE* it smiled a silent dell
Where the people did not dwell;
They had gone unto the wars,
Trusting to the mild-eyed stars,
Nightly, from their azure towers,
To keep watch above the flowers,
In the midst of which all day
The red sunlight lazily lay.
*Now* each visitor shall confess
The sad valley's restlessness.
Nothing there is motionless —
Nothing save the air's that brood
Over the magic solitude.
Ah, by no wind are stirred those trees
That palpitate like the chill seas
Around the misty Hebrides!
Ah, by no wind those clouds are driven
That rustle through the unquiet Heaven
Uneasily, from morn till even,
Over the violets there that lie
In myriad types of the human eye —
Over the lilies there that wave
And weep above a nameless grave!
They wave: — from out their fragrant tops
Eternal dews come down in drops.
They weep: — from off their delicate stems
Perennial tears descend in gems.

## THE CITY IN THE SEA.

LO! Death has reared himself a throne
In a strange city lying alone
Far down within the dim West,
Where the good and the bad and the worst and the best
Have gone to their eternal rest.
There shrines and palaces and towers
(Time-eaten towers that tremble not!)
Resemble nothing that is ours.
Around, by lifting winds forgot,
Resignedly beneath the sky
The melancholy waters lie.

No rays from the holy heaven come down
On the long night-time of that town;
But light from out the lurid sea
Streams up the turrets silently —
Gleams up the pinnacles far and free —
Up domes — up spires — up kingly halls —
Up fanes — up Babylon-like walls —
Up shadowy long-forgotten bowers
Of sculptured ivy and stone flowers —
Up many and many a marvellous shrine
Whose wreathèd friezes intertwine
The viol, the violet, and the vine.

Resignedly, beneath the sky
The melancholy waters lie.

So blend the turrets and shadows there
That all seem pendulous in air,
While, from a proud tower in the town,
Death looks gigantically down.

There open fanes and gaping graves
Yawn level with the luminous waves,
But not the riches there that lie
In each idol's diamond eye —
Not the gayly-jewelled dead
Tempt the waters from their bed;
For no ripples curl, alas!
Along that wilderness of glass —
No swellings tell that winds may be
Upon some far-off happier sea —
No heavings hint that winds have been
On scenes less hideously serene.

But low! a stir is in the air!
The wave — there is a movement there!
As if the towers had thrust aside,
In slightly sinking, the dull tide —
As if their tops had feebly given
A void within the filmy Heaven.
The waves have now a redder glow,
The hours are breathing faint and low —
And when, amid no earthly moans,
Down, down that town shall settle hence,
Hell, rising from a thousand thrones,
Shall do it reverence.

## THE SLEEPER.

AT midnight, in the month of June,
I stand beneath the mystic moon.
An opiate vapor, dewy, dim,
Exhales from out her golden rim,
And, softly dripping, drop by drop,
Upon the quiet mountain-top,
Steals drowsily and musically
Into the universal valley.
The rosemary nods upon the grave ;
The lily lolls upon the wave ;
Wrapping the fog about its breast,
The ruin moulders into rest ;
Looking like Lethe, see ! the lake
A conscious slumber seems to take,
And would not, for the world, awake.
All Beauty sleeps ! — and lo ! where lies
(Her casement open to the skies)
Irene, with her Destinies !
Oh, lady bright ! can it be right —
This window open to the night?
The wanton airs, from the tree-top,
Laughingly through the lattice drop —
The bodiless airs, a wizard rout,
Flit through thy chamber in and out,
And wave the curtain canopy
So fitfully — so fearfully —

Above the closed and fringed lid
'Neath which thy slumb'ring soul lies hid,
That, o'er the floor and down the wall,
Like ghosts the shadows rise and fall!
Oh, lady dear, hast thou no fear?
Why and what art thou dreaming here?
Sure thou art come o'er far-off seas,
A wonder to these garden trees!
Strange is thy pallor! strange thy dress!
Strange, above all, thy length of tress,
And this all solemn silentness!

The lady sleeps! Oh, may her sleep,
Which is enduring, so be deep!
Heaven have her in its sacred keep!
This chamber changed for one more holy,
This bed for one more melancholy,
I pray to God that she may lie
Forever with unopened eye,
While the dim sheeted ghosts go by!

My love, she sleeps! Oh, may her sleep,
As it is lasting, so be deep!
Soft may the worms about her creep!
Far in the forest, dim and old,
For her may some tall vault unfold —
Some vault that oft hath flung its black
And winged panels fluttering back,

Triumphant, o'er the crested palls
Of her grand family funerals —
Some sepulchre, remote, alone,
Against whose portal she hath thrown,
In childhood, many an idle stone —
Some tomb from out whose sounding door
She ne'er shall force an echo more,
Thrilling to think, poor child of sin!
It was the dead who groaned within.

---

## SILENCE.

THERE are some qualities — some incorporate things,
That have a double life, which thus is made
A type of that twin entity which springs
From matter and light, evinced in solid and shade.
There is a twofold *Silence* — sea and shore —
Body and soul. One dwells in lonely places,
Newly with grass o'ergrown; some solemn graces,
Some human memories and tearful lore,
Render him terrorless: his name 's "No More."
He is the corporate Silence: dread him not!
No power hath he of evil in himself;
But should some urgent fate (untimely lot!)
Bring thee to meet his shadow (nameless elf,
That haunteth the lone regions where hath trod
No foot of man), commend thyself to God!

## A DREAM WITHIN A DREAM.

TAKE this kiss upon the brow!
And, in parting from you now,
Thus much let me avow —
You are not wrong, who deem
That my days have been a dream;
Yet if hope has flown away
In a night, or in a day,
In a vision, or in none,
Is it therefore the less *gone?*
*All* that we see or seem
Is but a dream within a dream.

I stand amid the roar
Of a surf-tormented shore,
And I hold within my hand
Grains of the golden sand —
How few! yet how they creep
Through my fingers to the deep,
While I weep — while I weep!
O God! can I not grasp
Them with a tighter clasp?
O God! can I not save
*One* from the pitiless wave?
Is *all* that we see or seem
But a dream within a dream?

## DREAM-LAND.

BY a route obscure and lonely,
Haunted by ill angels only,
Where an Eidolon, named NIGHT,
On a black throne reigns upright,
I have reached these lands but newly
From an ultimate dim Thule —
From a wild weird clime that lieth, sublime,
Out of SPACE — out of TIME.

Bottomless vales and boundless floods,
And chasms, and caves, and Titan woods,
With forms that no man can discover
For the dews that drip all over;
Mountains toppling evermore
Into seas without a shore;
Seas that restlessly aspire,
Surging, unto skies of fire;
Lakes that endlessly outspread
Their lone waters — lone and dead, —
Their still waters — still and chilly
With the snows of the lolling lily.

By the lakes that thus outspread
Their lone waters, lone and dead, —
Their sad waters, sad and chilly
With the snows of the lolling lily, —

By the mountains — near the river
Murmuring lowly, murmuring ever, —
By the gray woods, —by the swamp
Where the toad and the newt encamp, —
By the dismal tarns and pools
  Where dwell the Ghouls, —
By each spot the most unholy —
In each nook most melancholy, —
There the traveller meets aghast
Sheeted Memories of the Past —
Shrouded forms that start and sigh
As they pass the wanderer by —
White-robed forms of friends long given,
In agony, to the Earth — and Heaven.

For the heart whose woes are legion
'T is a peaceful, soothing region —
For the spirit that walks in shadow
'T is — oh 't is an Eldorado!
But the traveller, travelling through it,
May not — dare not openly view it;
Never its mysteries are exposed
To the weak human eye unclosed;
So wills its King, who hath forbid
The uplifting of the fringed lid;
And thus the sad Soul that here passes
Beholds it but through darkened glasses.

By a route obscure and lonely,
Haunted by ill angels only,
Where an Eidolon, named NIGHT,
On a black throne reigns upright,
I have wandered home but newly
From this ultimate dim Thule.

---

## TO ZANTE.

FAIR isle, that from the fairest of all flowers,
Thy gentlest of all gentle names dost take!
How many memories of what radiant hours
At sight of thee and thine at once awake!
How many scenes of what departed bliss!
How many thoughts of what entombèd hopes!
How many visions of a maiden that is
No more — no more upon thy verdant slopes!
*No more!* alas, that magical sad sound
Transforming all! Thy charms shall please *no more*—
Thy memory *no more!* Accursèd ground
Henceforth I hold thy flower-enamelled shore,
O hyacinthine isle! O purple Zante!
"Isola d'oro! Fior di Levante!"

## EULALIE.

 DWELT alone
In a world of moan,
And my soul was a stagnant tide,
Till the fair and gentle Eulalie became my blushing bride —
Till the yellow-haired young Eulalie became my smiling bride.

Ah, less — less bright
The stars of the night
Than the eyes of the radiant girl;
And never a flake
That the vapor can make
With the moon-tints of purple and pearl,
Can vie with the modest Eulalie's most unregarded curl —
Can compare with the bright-eyed Eulalie's most humble and careless curl.

Now Doubt — now Pain
Come never again,
For her soul gives me sigh for sigh,
And all day long
Shines bright and strong,
Astarté within the sky,
While ever to her dear Eulalie upturns her matron eye —
While ever to her young Eulalie upturns her violet eye.

## ELDORADO.

GAYLY bedight,
A gallant knight,
In sunshine and in shadow,
Had journeyed long,
Singing a song,
In search of Eldorado.

But he grew old —
This knight so bold —
And o'er his heart a shadow
Fell as he found
No spot of ground
That looked like Eldorado.

And, as his strength
Failed him at length,
He met a pilgrim shadow —
" Shadow," said he,
" Where can it be —
This land of Eldorado?"

" Over the Mountains
Of the Moon,
Down the Valley of the Shadow,
Ride, boldly ride,"
The shade replied, —
" If you seek for Eldorado!"

## ISRAFEL.*

N Heaven a spirit doth dwell
"Whose heart-strings are a lute;"
None sing so wildly well
As the angel Israfel,
And the giddy stars (so legends tell)
Ceasing their hymns, attend the spell
Of his voice, all mute.

Tottering above
In her highest noon,
The enamored moon
Blushes with love,
While, to listen, the red levin
(With the rapid Pleiades, even,
Which were seven),
Pauses in Heaven.

And they say (the starry choir
And the other listening things)
That Israfeli's fire
Is owing to that lyre
By which he sits and sings —
The trembling living wire
Of those unusual strings.

---

* And the angel Israfel, whose heart-strings are a lute, and who has the sweetest voice of all God's creatures. — KORAN.

But the skies that angel trod,
  Where deep thoughts are a duty —
Where Love 's a grown-up God —
  Where the Houri glances are
Imbued with all the beauty
  Which we worship in a star.

Therefore, thou art not wrong,
  Israfeli, who despisest
An unimpassioned song;
To thee the laurels belong,
  Best bard, because the wisest!
Merrily live, and long!

The ecstasies above
  With thy burning measures suit —
Thy grief, thy joy, thy hate, thy love,
  With the fervor of thy lute —
  Well may the stars be mute!

Yes, Heaven is thine; but this
  Is a world of sweets and sours;
  Our flowers are merely — flowers,
And the shadow of thy perfect bliss
  Is the sunshine of ours.

If I could dwell
Where Israfel
  Hath dwelt, and he where I,

He might not sing so wildly well
  A mortal melody,
While a bolder note than this might swell
  From my lyre within the sky.

---

## FOR ANNIE.

THANK Heaven! the crisis —
  The danger is past,
And the lingering illness
  Is over at last —
And the fever called "Living"
  Is conquered at last.

Sadly, I know,
  I am shorn of my strength,
And no muscle I move
  As I lie at full length —
But no matter! — I feel
  I am better at length.

And I rest so composed
  Now, in my bed,
That any beholder
  Might fancy me dead —
Might start at beholding me,
  Thinking me dead.

The moaning and groaning,
  The sighing and sobbing
Are quieted now,
  With that horrible throbbing
At heart: — ah, that horrible,
  Horrible throbbing!

The sickness — the nausea —
  The pitiless pain —
Have ceased, with the fever
  That maddened my brain —
With the fever called "Living"
  That burned in my brain.

And oh! of all tortures
  *That* torture the worst
Has abated — the terrible
  Torture of thirst
For the napthaline river
  Of Passion accurst: —
I have drank of a water
  That quenches all thirst: —

Of a water that flows,
  With a lullaby sound,
From a spring but a very few
  Feet under ground —
From a cavern not very far
  Down under ground.

And ah! let it never
  Be foolishly said
That my room it is gloomy
  And narrow my bed;
For man never slept
  In a different bed —
And, to *sleep*, you must slumber
  In just such a bed.

My tantalized spirit
  Here blandly reposes,
Forgetting, or never
  Regretting its roses —
Its old agitations
  Of myrtles and roses:

For now, while so quietly
  Lying, it fancies
A holier odor
  About it, of pansies —
A rosemary odor,
  Commingled with pansies —
With rue and the beautiful
  Puritan pansies.

And so it lies happily,
  Bathing in many
A dream of the truth
  And the beauty of Annie —

Drowned in a bath
  Of the tresses of Annie.

She tenderly kissed me,
  She fondly caressed,
And then I fell gently
  To sleep on her breast —
Deeply to sleep
  From the heaven of her breast.

When the light was extinguished,
  She covered me warm,
And she prayed to the angels
  To keep me from harm —
To the queen of the angels
  To shield me from harm.

And I lie so composedly,
  Now, in my bed,
(Knowing her love)
  That you fancy me dead —
And I rest so contentedly,
  Now in my bed,
(With her love at my breast)
  That you fancy me dead —
That you shudder to look at me,
  Thinking me dead: —

But my heart it is brighter
  Than all of the many
Stars in the sky,
  For it sparkles with Annie —
It glows with the light
  Of the love of my Annie —
With the thought of the light
  Of the eyes of my Annie.

---

## TO ——.

I HEED not that my earthly lot
  Hath — little of Earth in it —
That years of love have been forgot
  In the hatred of a minute: —
I mourn not that the desolate
  Are happier, sweet, than I,
But that *you* sorrow for *my* fate
  Who am a passer-by.

---

## BRIDAL BALLAD.

THE ring is on my hand,
  And the wreath is on my brow;
Satins and jewels grand
Are all at my command,
  And I am happy now.

And my lord he loves me well;
  But, when first he breathed his vow,
I felt my bosom swell —
For the words rang as a knell,
And the voice seemed *his* who fell
In the battle down the dell,
  And who is happy now.

But he spoke to reassure me,
  And he kissed my pallid brow,
While a reverie came o'er me,
And to the church-yard bore me,
And I sighed to him before me,
Thinking him dead D'Elormie,
  "Oh, I am happy now!"

And thus the words were spoken,
  And this the plighted vow,
And, though my faith be broken,
And, though my heart be broken,
Behold the golden token
  That *proves* me happy now!

Would God I could awaken!
  For I dream I know not how,
And my soul is sorely shaken
Lest an evil step be taken, —
Lest the dead who is forsaken
  May not be happy now.

## TO F——.

BELOVED! amid the earnest woes
That crowd around my earthly path—
(Drear path, alas! where grows
Not even one lonely rose)—
My soul at least a solace hath
In dreams of thee, and therein knows
An Eden of bland repose.

And thus my memory is to me
Like some enchanted far-off isle
In some tumultuous sea—
Some ocean throbbing far and free
With storms—but where meanwhile
Serenest skies continually
Just o'er that one bright island smile.

# SCENES FROM "POLITIAN";

## AN UNPUBLISHED DRAMA.

### I.

ROME. — A Hall in a Palace. Alessandra and Castiglione.

*ALESSANDRA.* Thou art sad, Castiglione,
*Castiglione.* Sad! — not I.
Oh, I 'm the happiest, happiest man in Rome!
A few days more, thou knowest, my Alessandra,
Will make thee mine. Oh, I am very happy!
*Aless.* Methinks thou hast a singular way of showing
Thy happiness! — what ails thee, cousin of mine?
Why didst thou sigh so deeply?
*Cas.* Did I sigh?
I was not conscious of it. It is a fashion,
A silly — a most silly fashion I have
When I am *very* happy. Did I sigh? (*Sighing.*)
*Aless.* Thou didst. Thou art not well. Thou hast indulged
Too much of late, and I am vexed to see it.
Late hours and wine, Castiglione, — these
Will ruin thee! thou art already altered —
Thy looks are haggard — nothing so wears away
The constitution as late hours and wine.

*Cas.* (*musing*). Nothing, fair cousin, nothing — not even deep sorrow —
Wears it away like evil hours and wine.
I will amend.
*Aless.* Do it! I would have thee drop
Thy riotous company, too — fellows low born —
Ill suit the like with old Di Broglio's heir
And Alessandra's husband.
*Cas.* I will drop them.
*Aless.* Thou wilt — thou must. Attend thou also more
To thy dress and equipage — they are over plain
For thy lofty rank and fashion — much depends
Upon appearances.
*Cas.* I 'll see to it.
*Aless.* Then see to it! — pay more attention, sir,
To a becoming carriage — much thou wantest
In dignity.
*Cas.* Much, much, oh much I want
In proper dignity.
*Aless.* (*haughtily*). Thou mockest me, sir!
*Cas.* (*abstractedly*). Sweet, gentle Lalage!
*Aless.* Heard I aright?
I speak to him — he speaks of Lalage!
Sir Count! (*places her hand on his shoulder*) what art thou dreaming? he 's not well!
What ails thee, sir?

*Cas.* (*starting*). Cousin! fair cousin! — madam!
I crave thy pardon — indeed I am not well —
Your hand from off my shoulder, if you please.
This air is most oppressive! — Madam — the Duke!

*Enter Di Broglio.*

*Di Broglio.* My son, I've news for thee! — hey? — what 's the matter? (*observing Alessandra.*)
I' the pouts? Kiss her, Castiglione! kiss her,
You dog! and make it up, I say, this minute!
I 've news for you both. Politian is expected
Hourly in Rome — Politian, Earl of Leicester!
We 'll have him at the wedding. 'T is his first visit
To the imperial city.

*Aless.* What! Politian
Of Britain, Earl of Leicester?

*Di Brog.* The same, my love.
We 'll have him at the wedding. A man quite young
In years, but gray in fame. I have not seen him,
But Rumor speaks of him as of a prodigy
Pre-eminent in arts and arms, and wealth,
And high descent. We 'll have him at the wedding.

*Aless.* I have heard much of this Politian.
Gay, volatile, and giddy — is he not?
And little given to thinking.

*Di Brog.* Far from it, love.
No branch, they say, of all philosophy
So deep, abstruse he has not mastered it.
Learned as few are learned.

*Aless.* 'T is very strange!
I have known men have seen Politian
And sought his company. They speak of him
As of one who entered madly into life,
Drinking the cup of pleasure to the dregs.
*Cas.* Ridiculous! Now *I* have seen Politian
And know him well — nor learned nor mirthful he.
He is a dreamer and a man shut out
From common passions.
*Di Brog.* Children, we disagree.
Let us go forth and taste the fragrant air
Of the garden. Did I dream, or did I hear
Politian was a *melancholy* man? (*Exeunt.*)

II.

ROME. — A Lady's apartment, with a window open and looking into a garden. Lalage, in deep mourning, reading at a table on which lie some books and a hand mirror. In the background Jacinta (a servant-maid) leans carelessly upon a chair.

*Lal.* Jacinta! is it thou?
*Jac.* (*pertly*). Yes, ma'am, I 'm here.
*Lal.* I did not know, Jacinta, you were in waiting.
Sit down! — let not my presence trouble you —
Sit down! — for I am humble, most humble.
*Jac.* (*aside*). 'T is time.
(*Jacinta seats herself in a sidelong manner upon the chair, resting her elbows upon the back, and regarding her mistress with a contemptuous look. Lalage continues to read.*)

*Lal.* "It in another climate, so he said,
Bore a bright golden flower, but not i' this soil!"
(*Pauses — turns over some leaves, and resumes.*)
"No lingering winters there, nor snow, nor shower —
But Ocean ever to refresh mankind
Breathes the shrill spirit of the western wind."
Oh, beautiful! — most beautiful! — how like
To what my fevered soul doth dream of Heaven!
O happy land! (*pauses*). She died! — the maiden died!
O still more happy maiden who couldst die!
Jacinta!
(*Jacinta returns no answer, and Lalage presently resumes.*)
Again! a similar tale
Told of a beauteous dame beyond the sea!
Thus speaketh one Ferdinand in the words of the play,
"She died full young" — one Bossola answers him —
"I think not so — her infelicity
Seemed to have years too many" — Ah, luckless lady!
Jacinta! (*Still no answer.*)
Here 's a far sterner story
But like — oh, very like in its despair —
Of that Egyptian queen, winning so easily
A thousand hearts — losing at length her own.
She died. Thus endeth the history — and her maids
Lean over her and weep — two gentle maids

With gentle names — Eiros and Charmion!
Rainbow and dove! —— Jacinta!
*Jac.* (*pettishly*). Madam, what *is* it?
*Lal.* Wilt thou, my good Jacinta, be so kind
As go down in the library and bring me
The Holy Evangelists?
*Jac.* Pshaw! (*Exit.*)
*Lal.* If there be balm
For the wounded spirit in Gilead, it is there!
Dew in the night-time of my bitter trouble
Will there be found — "dew sweeter far than that
Which hangs like chains of pearl on Hermon hill."
(*Re-enter Jacinta, and throws a volume on the table.*)
There, ma'am, 's the book. (*Aside.*) Indeed she is very troublesome.
*Lal.* (*astonished*). What didst thou say, Jacinta? Have done aught
To grieve thee or to vex thee? — I am sorry.
For thou hast served me long and ever been
Trustworthy and respectful. (*Resumes her reading.*)
*Jac.* (*aside*). I can't believe
She has any more jewels — no — no— she gave me all.
*Lal.* What didst thou say, Jacinta? Now I bethink me
Thou hast not spoken lately of thy wedding.
How fares good Ugo? — and when is it to be?

Can I do aught! — is there no further aid
Thou needest, Jacinta?
*Jac.* (*aside*). Is there no *further* aid!
That 's meant for me. — I 'm sure, madam, you need not
Be always throwing those jewels in my teeth.
*Lal.* Jewels! Jacinta, — now indeed, Jacinta,
I thought not of the jewels.
*Jac.* Oh! perhaps not!
But then I might have sworn it. After all
There 's Ugo says the ring is only paste,
For he 's sure the Count Castiglione never
Would have given a real diamond to such as you;
And at the best I 'm certain, madam, you cannot
Have use for jewels *now*. But I might have sworn it.
(*Exit.*)
(*Lalage bursts into tears and leans her head upon the table — after a short pause raises it.*)
*Lal.* Poor Lalage! — and is it to come to this?
Thy servant-maid! — but courage! — 't is but a viper
Who thou hast cherished to sting thee to the soul!
(*Taking up the mirror.*)
Ha! here at least 's a friend — too much a friend
In earlier days — a friend will not deceive thee
Fair mirror and true! now tell me (for thou canst)
A tale — a pretty tale — and heed thou not
Though it be rife with woe. It answers me.
It speaks of sunken eyes, and wasted cheeks,

And Beauty long deceased — remembers me
Of Joy departed — Hope, the Seraph Hope,
Inurned and intombed! now, in a tone
Low, sad, and solemn, but most audible,
Whispers of early grave untimely yawning
For ruined maid. Fair mirror and true! — thou liest
not!
*Thou* hast no end to gain — no heart to break —
Castiglione lied who said he loved ——
Thou true — he false! — false! — false!

(*While she speaks, a monk enters her apartment, and approaches unobserved.*)

*Monk.* Refuge thou hast,
Sweet daughter! in Heaven. Think of eternal things!
Give up thy soul to penitence, and pray!

*Lal.* (*arising hurriedly*). I *cannot* pray! — My soul is at war with God!
The frightful sounds of merriment below
Disturb my senses — go! I cannot pray —
The sweet airs from the garden worry me!
Thy presence grieves me — go! — thy priestly raiment
Fills me with dread — thy ebony crucifix
With horror and awe!

*Monk.* Think of thy precious soul!

*Lal.* Think of my early days! — think of my father
And mother in Heaven! think of our quiet home,
And the rivulet that ran before the door!

Think of my little sisters ! — think of them !
And think of me ! — think of my trusting love
And confidence — his vows — my ruin — think — think
Of my unspeakable misery ! —— begone !
Yet stay ! yet stay ! — what was it thou saidst of prayer
And penitence ? Didst thou not speak of faith
And vows before the throne ?
*Monk.* I did.
*Lal.* 'T is well.
There *is* a vow were fitting should be made —
A sacred vow, imperative and urgent,
A solemn vow !
*Monk.* Daughter, this zeal is well !
*Lal.* Father, this zeal is anything but well !
Hast thou a crucifix fit for this thing ?
A crucifix whereon to register
This sacred vow ? (*He hands her his own.*)
Not that — Oh ! no ! — no ! — no ! (*Shuddering.*)
Not that ! Not that ! — I tell thee, holy man,
Thy raiments and thy ebony cross affright me !
Stand back ! I have a crucifix myself, —
*I* have a crucifix ! Methinks 't were fitting
The deed — the vow — the symbol of the deed —
And the deed's register should tally, father !
(*Draws a cross-handled dagger and raises it on high.*)
Behold the cross wherewith a vow like mine
Is written in Heaven !

*Monk.* Thy words are madness, daughter,
And speak a purpose unholy — thy lips are livid —
Thine eyes are wild — tempt not the wrath divine!
Pause ere too late! — Oh be not — be not rash!
Swear not the oath — oh swear it not!
*Lal.* 'T is sworn!

## III.

An apartment in a palace. Politian and Baldazzar.

*Baldazzar.* — Arouse thee now, Politian!
Thou must not — nay indeed, indeed, thou shalt not
Give way unto these humors. Be thyself!
Shake off the idle fancies that beset thee,
And live, for now thou diest!
*Politian.* Not so, Baldazzar!
*Surely* I live.
*Bal.* Politian, it doth grieve me
To see thee thus.
*Pol.* Baldazzar, it doth grieve me
To give thee cause for grief, my honored friend.
Command me, sir! what wouldst thou have me do?
At thy behest I will shake off that nature
Which from my forefathers I did inherit,
Which with my mother's milk I did imbibe,
And be no more Politian, but some other.
Command me, sir!

*Bal.* To the field, then — to the field —
To the senate or the field.
*Pol.* Alas! alas!
There is an imp would follow me even there!
There is an imp *hath* followed me even there!
There is —— what voice was that?
*Bal.* I heard it not.
I heard not any voice except thine own,
And the echo of thine own.
*Pol.* Then I but dreamed.
*Bal.* Give not thy soul to dreams: the camp — the court
Befit thee — Fame awaits thee — Glory calls —
And her the trumpet-tongued thou wilt not hear
In hearkening to imaginary sounds
And phantom voices.
*Pol.* It *is* a phantom voice!
Didst thou not hear it *then?*
*Bal.* I heard it not.
*Pol.* Thou heardst it not! — Baldazzar, speak no more
To me, Politian, of thy camps and courts.
Oh! I am sick, sick, sick, even unto death,
Of the hollow and high-sounding vanities
Of the populous Earth! Bear with me yet awhile!
We have been boys together — school-fellows —
And now are friends — yet shall not be so long —

For in the eternal city thou shalt do me
A kind and gentle office, and a Power —
A Power august, benignant, and supreme —
Shall then absolve thee of all further duties
Unto thy friend.
*Bal.* Thou speakest a fearful riddle
I *will* not understand.
*Pol.* Yet now as Fate
Approaches, and the Hours are breathing low,
The sands of Time are changed to golden grains,
And dazzle me, Baldazzar. Alas! alas!
I *cannot* die, having within my heart
So keen a relish for the beautiful
As hath been kindled within it. Methinks the air
Is balmier now than it was wont to be —
Rich melodies are floating in the winds —
A rarer loveliness bedecks the earth —
And with a holier lustre the quiet moon
Sitteth in Heaven. — Hist! hist! thou canst not say
Thou hearest not *now*, Baldazzar?
*Bal.* Indeed I hear not.
*Pol.* Not hear it? — listen now — listen! — the faintest sound
And yet the sweetest that ear ever heard!
A lady's voice! — and sorrow in the tone!
Baldazzar, it oppresses me like a spell!
Again! — again! — how solemnly it falls

Into my heart of hearts! that eloquent voice
Surely I never heard — yet it were well
Had I *but* heard it with its thrilling tones
In earlier days!

*Bal.* I myself hear it now.
Be still! — the voice, if I mistake not greatly,
Proceeds from yonder lattice — which you may see
Very plainly through the window — it belongs,
Does it not? unto this palace of the Duke.
The singer is undoubtedly beneath
The roof of his Excellency — and perhaps
Is even that Alessandra of whom he spake
As the betrothed of Castiglione,
His son and heir.

*Pol.* Be still! — it comes again!

*Voice (very faintly).* "And is thy heart so strong
As for to leave me thus
Who hath loved thee so long
In wealth and woe among?
And is thy heart so strong
As for to leave me thus?
Say nay — say nay!"

*Bal.* The song is English, and I oft have heard it
In merry England — never so plaintively —
Hist! hist! it comes again!

*Voice* (*more loudly*).
"Is it so strong
As for to leave me thus
Who hath loved thee so long
In wealth and woe among?
And is thy heart so strong
As for to leave me thus?
Say nay — say nay!"

*Bal.* 'T is hushed and all is still!

*Pol.* All *is not* still.

*Bal.* Let us go down.

*Pol.* Go down, Baldazzar, go!

*Bal.* The hour is growing late — the Duke awaits us, —
Thy presence is expected in the hall
Below. What ails thee, Earl Politian?

*Voice* (*distinctly*).
"Who hath loved thee so long,
In wealth and woe among,
And is thy heart so strong?
Say nay — say nay!"

*Bal.* Let us descend! — 't is time. Politian, give
These fancies to the wind. Remember, pray,
Your bearing lately savored much of rudeness
Unto the Duke. Arouse thee! and remember!

*Pol.* Remember? I do. Lead on! I *do* remember.
(*Going.*)
Let us descend. Believe me I would give,

Freely would give the broad lands of my earldom
To look upon the face hidden by yon lattice —
"To gaze upon that veiled face, and hear
Once more that silent tongue."
*Bal.* Let me beg you, sir,
Descend with me — the Duke may be offended.
Let us go down, I pray you.
*Voice* (*loudly*). *Say nay! — say nay!*
*Pol.* (*aside*). 'T is strange! — 't is very strange — methought the voice
Chimed in with my desires and bade me stay!
(*Approaching the window.*)
Sweet voice! I heed thee, and will surely stay.
Now be this Fancy, by Heaven, or be it Fate,
Still will I not descend. Baldazzar, make
Apology unto the Duke for me;
I go not down to-night.
*Bal.* Your lordship's pleasure
Shall be attended to. Good-night, Politian.
*Pol.* Good-night, my friend, good-night.

## IV.

The gardens of a palace — Moonlight. Lalage and Politian.

*Lalage.* And dost thou speak of love
To *me*, Politian? dost thou speak of love

To Lalage? — ah woe — ah woe is me!
This mockery is most cruel — most cruel indeed!
*Politian.* Weep not! oh, sob not thus! — thy bitter tears
Will madden me. Oh, mourn not, Lalage —
Be comforted! I know — I know it all,
And *still* I speak of love. Look at me, brightest,
And beautiful Lalage! turn here thine eyes!
Thou askest me if I could speak of love,
Knowing what I know, and seeing what I have seen.
Thou askest me that — and thus I answer thee —
Thus on my bended knee I answer thee.
(*Kneeling.*)
Sweet Lalage, *I love thee — love thee — love thee;*
Thro' good and ill — thro' weal and woe I *love thee.*
Not mother, with her first-born on her knee,
Thrills with intenser love than I for thee.
Not on God's altar, in any time or clime,
Burned there a holier fire than burneth now
Within my spirit for *thee.* And do I love?
(*Arising.*)
Even for thy woes I love thee — even for thy woes —
Thy beauty and thy woes.
*Lal.* Alas, proud Earl,
Thou dost forget thyself, remembering me!
How, in thy father's halls, among the maidens
Pure and reproachless of thy princely line,

Could the dishonored Lalage abide?
Thy wife, and with a tainted memory —
My seared and blighted name, how would it tally
With the ancestral honors of thy house,
And with thy glory?

*Pol.* Speak not to me of glory!
I hate — I loathe the name; I do abhor
The unsatisfactory and ideal thing.
Art thou not Lalage and I Politian?
Do I not love? — art thou not beautiful? —
What need we more? Ha! glory! — now speak not of it
By all I hold most sacred and most solemn —
By all my wishes now — my fears hereafter —
By all I scorn on earth and hope in heaven —
There is no deed I would more glory in,
Than in thy cause to scoff at this same glory
And trample it under foot. What matters it —
What matters it, my fairest, and my best,
That we go down unhonored and forgotten
Into the dust — so we descend together?
Descend together — and then — and then perchance —

*Lal.* Why dost thou pause, Politian?

*Pol.* And then perchance
*Arise* together, Lalage, and roam
The starry and quiet dwellings of the blest,
And still —

*Lal.* Why dost thou pause, Politian?

*Pol.* And still *together* — *together.*
*Lal.* Now, Earl of Leicester!
Thou *lovest* me, and in my heart of hearts
I feel thou lovest me truly.
*Pol.* Oh, Lalage! (*Throwing himself upon his knee.*)
And lovest thou *me?*
*Lal.* Hist! hush! Within the gloom
Of yonder trees methought a figure past —
A spectral figure, solemn, and slow, and noiseless —
Like the grim shadow Conscience, solemn and noiseless.
(*Walks across and returns.*)
I was mistaken — 't was but a giant bough
Stirred by the autumn wind. Politian!
*Pol.* My Lalage — my love! why art thou moved?
Why dost thou turn so pale? Not Conscience' self,
Far less a shadow which thou likenest to it,
Should shake the firm spirit thus. But the night-wind
Is chilly — and these melancholy boughs
Throw over all things a gloom.
*Lal.* Politian!
Thou speakest to me of love. Knowest thou the land
With which all tongues are busy — a land new found —
Miraculously found by one of Genoa —
A thousand leagues within the golden west?
A fairy land of flowers, and fruit, and sunshine,
And crystal lakes, and over-arching forests, [winds
And mountains, around whose towering summits the

Of Heaven untrammelled flow — which air to breathe
Is Happiness now, and will be Freedom hereafter
In days that are to come?
*Pol.* O, wilt thou — wilt thou
Fly to that Paradise — my Lalage, wilt thou
Fly thither with me? There Care shall be forgotten,
And Sorrow shall be no more, and Eros be all.
And life shall then be mine, for I will live
For thee, and in thine eyes — and thou shalt be
No more a mourner — but the radiant Joys
Shall wait upon thee, and the angel Hope
Attend thee ever; and I will kneel to thee
And worship thee, and call thee my beloved,
My own, my beautiful, my love, my wife,
My all; — oh, wilt thou — wilt thou, Lalage,
Fly thither with me?
*Lal.* A deed is to be done —
Castiglione lives!
*Pol.* And he shall die! (*Exit.*)
*Lal.* (*after a pause*). And — he — shall — die — alas!
Castiglione die? Who spoke the words?
Where am I? — what was it he said? — Politian!
Thou *art* not gone — thou art not *gone*, Politian!
I *feel* thou art not gone — yet dare not look,
Lest I behold thee not; thou *couldst* not go
With those words upon thy lips — O, speak to me!
And let me hear thy voice — one word — one word,

To say thou art not gone, — one little sentence,
To say how thou dost scorn — how thou dost hate
My womanly weakness. Ha! ha! thou *art* not gone —
O speak to me! I *knew* thou wouldst not go!
I knew thou wouldst not, couldst not, *durst* not go.
Villain, thou *art* not gone — thou mockest me!
And thus I clutch thee — thus! —— He is gone, he is gone —
Gone — gone. Where am I? — 't is well — 't is very well!
So that the blade be keen — the blow be sure,
'T is well, 't is *very* well — alas! alas!

## V.

The suburbs. Politian alone.

*Politian.* This weakness grows upon me. I am faint,
And much I fear me ill — it will not do
To die ere I have lived! — Stay — stay thy hand,
O Azrael, yet awhile! — Prince of the Powers
Of Darkness and the Tomb, O pity me!
O pity me! let me not perish now,
In the budding of my Paradisal Hope!
Give me to live yet — yet a little while:
'T is I who pray for life — I who so late
Demanded but to die! — what sayeth the Count?

*Enter Baldazzar.*

*Baldazzar.* That knowing no cause of quarrel or of feud
Between the Earl Politian and himself,
He doth decline your cartel.
*Pol.* *What* didst thou say?
What answer was it you brought me, good Baldazzar?
With what excessive fragrance the zephyr comes
Laden from yonder bowers! — a fairer day,
Or one more worthy Italy, methinks
No mortal eyes have seen! — *what* said the Count?
*Bal.* That he, Castiglione, not being aware
Of any feud existing, or any cause
Of quarrel between your lordship and himself,
Cannot accept the challenge.
*Pol.* It is most true —
All this is very true. When saw you, sir,
When saw you now, Baldazzar, in the frigid
Ungenial Britain which we left so lately,
A heaven so calm as this — so utterly free
From the evil taint of clouds? — and he did *say?*
*Bal.* No more, my lord, than I have told you, sir:
The Count Castiglione will not fight,
Having no cause or quarrel.
*Pol.* Now this is true —
All very true. Thou art my friend, Baldazzar,
And I have not forgotten it — thou 'lt do me
A piece of service; wilt thou go back and say

Unto this man, that I, the Earl of Leicester,
Hold him a villain? — thus much, I prythee, say
Unto the Count — it is exceeding just
He should have cause for quarrel.

*Bal.* My lord! — my friend —

*Pol.* (*aside*). 'T is he — he comes himself! (*Aloud.*)
Thou reasonest well.
I know what thou wouldst say — not send the message —
Well! — I will think of it — I will not send it.
Now prithee, leave me — hither doth come a person
With whom affairs of a most private nature
I would adjust.

*Bal.* I go — to-morrow we meet,
Do we not? — at the Vatican.

*Pol.* At the Vatican. (*Exit Bal.*)

*Enter Castiglione.*

*Cas.* The Earl of Leicester here!

*Pol.* I *am* the Earl of Leicester, and thou seest,
Dost thou not? that I am here.

*Cas.* My lord, some strange,
Some singular mistake — misunderstanding —
Hath without doubt arisen: thou hast been urged
Thereby, in heat of anger, to address
Some words most unaccountable, in writing,
To me, Castiglione; the bearer being
Baldazzar, Duke of Surrey. I am aware
Of nothing which might warrant thee in this thing,

Having given thee no offence. Ha! — am I right?
'T was a mistake? — undoubtedly — we all
Do err at times.

*Pol.* Draw, villain, and prate no more!

*Cas.* Ha! — draw! — and villain! have at thee then at once,
Proud Earl! (*Draws.*)

*Pol.* (*drawing*). Thus to the expiatory tomb,
Untimely sepulchre, I do devote thee
In the name of Lalage!

*Cas.* (*letting fall his sword and recoiling to the extremity of the stage*).
Of Lalage!
Hold off — thy sacred hand! — avaunt I say!
Avaunt — I will not fight thee — indeed I dare not.

*Pol.* Thou wilt not fight with me didst say, Sir Count?
Shall I be baffled thus? — now this is well;
Didst say thou *darest* not? Ha!

*Cas.* I dare not — dare not —
Hold off thy hand — with that beloved name
So fresh upon thy lips I will not fight thee —
I cannot — dare not.

*Pol.* Now by my halidom
I do believe thee! — coward, I do believe thee!

*Cas.* Ha! — coward! — this may not be!

(*Clutches his sword, and staggers towards Politian, but his purpose is changed before reaching him, and he falls upon his knee at the feet of the Earl.*)

Alas! my lord,
It is — it is — most true. In such a cause
I am the veriest coward. O pity me! [thee.
*Pol.* (*greatly softened*). Alas! — I do — indeed I pity
*Cas.* And Lalage —
*Pol.* *Scoundrel! — arise and die!*
*Cas.* It needeth not be — thus — thus — O let me die
Thus on my bended knee. It were most fitting
That in this deep humiliation I perish.
For in the fight I will not raise a hand
Against thee, Earl of Leicester. Strike thou home —
(*baring his bosom*).
Here is no let or hinderance to thy weapon —
Strike home. I *will* not fight thee.
*Pol.* Now s'Death and Hell!
Am I not — am I not sorely — grievously tempted
To take thee at thy word? But mark me, sir:
Think not to fly me thus. Do thou prepare
For public insult in the streets — before
The eyes of the citizens. I 'll follow thee —
Like an avenging spirit I 'll follow thee
Even unto death. Before those whom thou lovest —
Before all Rome I 'll taunt thee, villain — I 'll taunt thee,
Dost hear? with *cowardice* — thou *wilt not* fight me?
Thou liest! thou *shalt!* (*Exit.*)
*Cas.* Now this indeed is just!
Most righteous, and most just, avenging Heaven.

## POEMS WRITTEN IN YOUTH.*

### SONNET — TO SCIENCE.

SCIENCE! true daughter of Old Time thou art!
Who alterest all things with thy peering eyes.
Why preyest thou thus upon the poet's heart,
Vulture, whose wings are dull realities?
How should he love thee? or how deem thee wise,
Who wouldst not leave him in his wandering
To seek for treasure in the jewelled skies,
Albeit he soared with an undaunted wing?
Hast thou not dragged Diana from her car?
And driven the Hamadryad from the wood
To seek a shelter in some happier star?
Hast thou not torn the Naiad from her flood,
The Elfin from the green grass, and from me
The summer dream beneath the tamarind tree?

---

* Private reasons — some of which have reference to the sin of plagiarism, and others to the date of Tennyson's first poems — have induced me, after some hesitation, to republish these, the crude compositions of my earliest boyhood. They are printed *verbatim*, without alteration from the original edition, the date of which is too remote to be judiciously acknowledged. E. A. P.

# AL AARAAF.*

## PART I.

! NOTHING earthly save the ray
(Thrown back from flowers) of Beauty's eye,
As in those gardens where the day
Springs from the gems of Circassy —
O! nothing earthly save the thrill
Of melody in woodland rill —
Or (music of the passion-hearted)
Joy's voice so peacefully departed
That like the murmur in the shell,
Its echo dwelleth and will dwell —
O! nothing of the dross of ours —
Yet all the beauty — all the flowers
That list our Love, and deck our bowers —
Adorn yon world afar, afar —
The wandering star.

'T was a sweet time for Nesace — for there
Her world lay lolling on the golden air,
Near four bright suns — a temporary rest —
An oasis in desert of the blest.

---

* A star was discovered by Tycho Brahe, which appeared suddenly in the heavens; attained, in a few days, a brilliancy surpassing that of Jupiter; then as suddenly disappeared, and has never been seen since.

Away — away — 'mid seas of rays that roll
Empyrean splendor o'er the unchained soul —
The soul that scarce (the billows are so dense)
Can struggle to its destin'd eminence —
To distant spheres, from time to time, she rode,
And late to ours, the favor'd one of God —
But, now, the ruler of an anchor'd realm,
She throws aside the sceptre — leaves the helm,
And, amid incense and high spiritual hymns,
Laves in quadruple light her angel limbs.

Now happiest, loveliest in yon lovely Earth,
Whence sprang the "Idea of Beauty" into birth,
(Falling in wreaths thro' many a startled star,
Like woman's hair 'mid pearls, until, afar,
It lit on hills Achaian, and there dwelt)
She look'd into Infinity — and knelt.
Rich clouds, for canopies, about her curled —
Fit emblems of the model of her world —
Seen but in beauty — not impeding sight
Of other beauty glittering thro' the light —
A wreath that twined each starry form around,
And all the opal'd air in color bound.

All hurriedly she knelt upon a bed
Of flowers: of lilies such as rear'd the head
On the fair Capo Deucato,* and sprang
So eagerly around about to hang

* On Santa Maura — olim Deucadia.

Upon the flying footsteps of — deep pride —
Of her who lov'd a mortal — and so died.*
The Sephalica, budding with young bees,
Uprear'd its purple stem around her knees:
And gemmy flower, of Trebizond misnam'd † —
Inmate of highest stars, where erst it sham'd
All other loveliness: its honied dew
(The fabled nectar that the heathen knew)
Deliriously sweet, was dropp'd from Heaven,
And fell on gardens of the unforgiven
In Trebizond — and on a sunny flower
So like its own above that, to this hour,
It still remaineth, torturing the bee
With madness, and unwonted reverie:
In Heaven, and all its environs, the leaf
And blossom of the fairy plant, in grief
Disconsolate linger — grief that hangs her head,
Repenting follies that full long have fled,
Heaving her white breast to the balmy air,
Like guilty beauty, chasten'd, and more fair:
Nyctanthes too, as sacred as the light
She fears to perfume, perfuming the night:
And Clytia ‡ pondering between many a sun,
While pettish tears adown her petals run:

---

* Sappho.

† This flower is much noticed by Lewenhoeck and Tournefort. The bee, feeding upon its blossom, becomes intoxicated.

‡ Clytia, — the Chrysanthemum Peruvianum, or, to employ a better-known term, the Turnsol, — which turns continually towards the sun, covers itself, like

And that aspiring flower that sprang on Earth
And died, ere scarce exalted into birth,*
Bursting its odorous heart in spirit to wing
Its way to Heaven, from garden of a king:
And Valisnerian lotus † thither flown
From struggling with the waters of the Rhone:
And thy most lovely purple perfume, Zante! ‡
Isola d'oro! Fior di Levante!
And the Nelumbo bud § that floats for ever
With Indian Cupid down the holy river —
Fair flowers, and fairy! to whose care is given
To bear the Goddess' song in odors, up to Heaven: ‖
"Spirit! that dwellest where,
In the deep sky,
The terrible and fair,
In beauty vie!

---

Peru, the country from which it comes, with dewy clouds which cool and refresh its flowers during the most violent heat of the day. — *B. de St. Pierre.*

* There is cultivated in the king's garden at Paris a species of serpentine aloes without prickles, whose large and beautiful flower exhales a strong odor of the vanilla, during the time of its expansion, which is very short. It does not blow till towards the month of July: you then perceive it gradually open its petals, expand them, fade and die. — *St. Pierre.*

† There is found, in the Rhone, a beautiful lily of the Valisnerian kind. Its stem will stretch to the length of three or four feet, thus preserving its head above water in the swellings of the river.

‡ The Hyacinth.

§ It is a fiction of the Indians, that Cupid was first seen floating in one of these down the river Ganges, and that he still loves the cradle of his childhood.

‖ And golden vials full of odors which are the prayers of the saints. — *Rev. St. John.*

Beyond the line of blue —
   The boundary of the star
Which turneth at the view
   Of thy barrier and thy bar —
Of the barrier overgone
   By the comets who were cast
From their pride, and from their throne
   To be drudges till the last —
To be carriers of fire
   (The red fire of their heart)
With speed that may not tire
   And with pain that shall not part —
Who livest — *that* we know —
   In Eternity — we feel —
But the shadow of whose brow
   What spirit shall reveal?
Thro' the beings whom thy Nesace,
   Thy messenger hath known
Have dream'd for thy Infinity
   A model of their own* —

---

* The Humanitarians held that God was to be understood as having really a human form. — *Vide Clarke's Sermons*, vol. 1, page 26, fol. edit.

The drift of Milton's argument leads him to employ language which would appear, at first sight, to verge upon their doctrine; but it will be seen immediately, that he guards himself against the charge of having adopted one of the most ignorant errors of the dark ages of the church. — *Dr. Sumner's Notes on Milton's Christian Doctrine.*

This opinion, in spite of many testimonies to the contrary, could never have been very general. Andeus, a Syrian of Mesopotamia, was condemned for the

Thy will is done, O God!
  The star hath ridden high
Thro' many a tempest, but she rode
  Beneath thy burning eye;
And here, in thought, to thee —
  In thought that can alone
Ascend thy empire and so be
  A partner of thy throne —
By winged Fantasy,*
  My embassy is given,
Till secrecy shall knowledge be
  In the environs of Heaven."
She ceas'd — and buried then her burning cheek
Abash'd amid the lilies there, to seek
A shelter from the fervor of His eye;
For the stars trembled at the Deity.
She stirr'd not — breath'd not — for a voice was there
How solemnly pervading the calm air!

---

opinion, as heretical. He lived in the beginning of the fourth century. His disciples were called Anthropomorphites. — *Vide Du Pin.*

Among Milton's minor poems are these lines:

Dicite sacrorum præsides nemorum Deæ, etc.
Quis ille primus cujus ex imagine
Natura solers finxit humanum genus?
Eternus, incorruptus, æquævus polo,
Unusque et universus exemplar Dei. — And afterwards,
Non cui profundum Cæcitas lumen dedit
Dircæus augur vidit hunc alto sinu, etc.

* Seltsamen Tochter Jovis
Seinem Schosskinde
Der Phantasie. — *Goethe.*

A sound of silence on the startled ear
Which dreamy poets name "the music of the sphere."
Ours is a world of words: Quiet we call
"Silence" — which is the merest word of all.
All Nature speaks, and ev'n ideal things
Flap shadowy sounds from visionary wings —
But ah! not so when, thus, in realms on high
The eternal voice of God is passing by,
And the red winds are withering in the sky!

"What tho' in worlds which sightless* cycles run,
Link'd to a little system, and one sun —
Where all my love is folly, and the crowd
Still think my terrors but the thunder-cloud,
The storm, the earthquake, and the ocean-wrath —
(Ah! will they cross me in my angrier path?)
What tho' in worlds which own a single sun
The sands of Time grow dimmer as they run,
Yet thine is my resplendency, so given
To bear my secrets thro' the upper Heaven,
Leave tenantless thy crystal home, and fly,
With all thy train, athwart the moony sky —
Apart — like fire-flies † in Sicilian night,
And wing to other worlds another light!
Divulge the secrets of thy embassy
To the proud orbs that twinkle — and so be

* Sightless — too small to be seen. — *Legge.*

† I have often noticed a peculiar movement of the fire-flies. They will collect in a body and fly off, from a common centre, into innumerable radii.

To ev'ry heart a barrier and a ban
Lest the stars totter in the guilt of man!"

Up rose the maiden in the yellow night,
The single-mooned eve! — on Earth we plight
Our faith to one love — and one moon adore —
The birthplace of young Beauty had no more.
As sprang that yellow star from downy hours,
Up rose the maiden from her shrine of flowers,
And bent o'er sheeny mountain and dim plain
Her way — but left not yet her Therasæan* reign.

## PART II.

High on a mountain of enamell'd head —
Such as the drowsy shepherd on his bed
Of giant pasturage lying at his ease,
Raising his heavy eyelid, starts and sees
With many a mutter'd "hope to be forgiven"
What time the moon is quadrated in Heaven —
Of rosy head, that towering far away
Into the sunlit ether, caught the ray
Of sunken suns at eve — at noon of night,
While the moon danc'd with the fair stranger light —

---

* Therasæa, or Therasea, the island mentioned by Seneca, which, in a moment, arose from the sea to the eyes of astonished mariners.

Uprear'd upon such height arose a pile
Of gorgeous columns on th' unburthen'd air,
Flashing from Parian marble that twin smile
Far down upon the wave that sparkled there,
And nursled the young mountain in its lair.
Of molten stars* their pavement, such as fall
Thro' the ebon air, besilvering the pall
Of their own dissolution, while they die —
Adorning then the dwellings of the sky.
A dome, by linked light from Heaven let down,
Sat gently on these columns as a crown —
A window of one circular diamond, there,
Look'd out above into the purple air,
And rays from God shot down that meteor chain
And hallow'd all the beauty twice again,
Save when, between th' Empyrean and that ring,
Some eager spirit flapp'd his dusky wing.
But on the pillars Seraph eyes have seen
The dimness of this world: that grayish green
That Nature loves the best for Beauty's grave
Lurk'd in each cornice, round each architrave —
And every sculptur'd cherub thereabout
That from his marble dwelling peerèd out,
Seem'd earthly in the shadow of his niche —
Achaian statues in a world so rich?

---

* Some star which, from the ruin'd roof
Of shak'd Olympus, by mischance did fall. — *Milton.*

Friezes from Tadmor and Persepolis *—
From Balbec, and the stilly, clear abyss
Of beautiful Gomorrah ! † Oh ! the wave
Is now upon thee — but too late to save !

Sound loves to revel in a summer night:
Witness the murmur of the gray twilight
That stole upon the ear, in Eyraco,‡
Of many a wild star-gazer long ago —
That stealeth ever on the ear of him
Who, musing, gazeth on the distance dim.
And sees the darkness coming as a cloud —
Is not its form — its voice — most palpable and loud ? §

But what is this ? — it cometh — and it brings
A music with it — 't is the rush of wings —

* Voltaire, in speaking of Persepolis, says, "Je connois bien l'admiration qu'inspirent ces ruines — mais un palais erigé au pied d'une chaine des rochers sterils — peut il être un chef d'œuvre des arts!"

† "Oh! the wave"—Ula Deguisi is the Turkish appellation; but, on its own shores, it is called Bahar Loth, or Almotanah. There were undoubtedly more than two cities engulfed in the "dead sea." In the valley of Siddim were five, — Adrah, Zeboin, Zoar, Sodom, and Gomorrah. Stephen of Byzantium mentions eight, and Strabo thirteen (engulfed) — but the last is out of all reason.

It is said [Tacitus, Strabo, Josephus, Daniel of St. Saba, Nau, Maundrell, Troilo, D'Arvieux] that after an excessive drought, the vestiges of columns, walls, etc , are seen above the surface. At *any* season, such remains may be discovered by looking down into the transparent lake, and at such distances as would argue the existence of many settlements in the space now usurped by the "Asphaltites."

‡ Eyraco — Chaldea.

§ I have often thought I could distinctly hear the sound of the darkness as it stole over the horizon.

A pause — and then a sweeping, falling strain
And Nesace is in her halls again.
From the wild energy of wanton haste
  Her cheeks were flushing, and her lips apart;
And zone that clung around her gentle waist
  Had burst beneath the heaving of her heart.
Within the centre of that hall to breathe
She paus'd and panted, Zanthe! all beneath,
The fairy light that kiss'd her golden hair
And long'd to rest, yet could but sparkle there!

Young flowers * were whispering in melody
To happy flowers that night — and tree to tree;
Fountains were gushing music as they fell
In many a star-lit grove, or moon-lit dell;
Yet silence came upon material things —
Fair flowers, bright waterfalls, and angel wings —
And sound alone that from the spirit sprang
Bore burthen to the charm the maiden sang: —

"'Neath blue-bell or streamer —
  Or tufted wild spray
That keeps, from the dreamer,
  The moonbeam away † —

---

* Fairies use flowers for their charactery. — *Merry Wives of Windsor.*

† In Scripture is this passage: "The sun shall not harm thee by day, nor the moon by night." It is perhaps not generally known that the moon, in Egypt, has the effect of producing blindness to those who sleep with the face exposed to its rays, to which circumstance the passage evidently alludes.

Bright beings! that ponder,
  With half-closing eyes,
On the stars which your wonder
  Hath drawn from the skies,
Till they glance thro' the shade, and
  Come down to your brow
Like — eyes of the maiden
  Who calls on you now —
Arise! from your dreaming
  In violet bowers,
To duty beseeming
  These star-litten hours —
And shake from your tresses
  Encumber'd with dew
The breath of those kisses
  That cumber them too —
(O! how, without you, Love!
  Could angels be blest?)
Those kisses of true love
  That lull'd ye to rest!
Up! shake from your wing
  Each hindering thing:
The dew of the night —
  It would weigh down your flight;
And true love caresses —
  O! leave them apart!
They are light on the tresses,
  But lead on the heart.

Ligeia! Ligeia!
  My beautiful one!
Whose harshest idea
  Will to melody run,
O! is it thy will
  On the breezes to toss?
Or, capriciously still,
  Like the lone Albatross,*
Incumbent on night
  (As she on the air)
To keep watch with delight
  On the harmony there?

"Ligeia! wherever
  Thy image may be,
No magic shall sever
  Thy music from thee.
Thou hast bound many eyes
  In a dreamy sleep —
But the strains still arise
  Which *thy* vigilance keep —
The sound of the rain
  Which leaps down to the flower,
And dances again
  In the rhythm of the shower —

---

* The Albatross is said to sleep on the wing.

The murmur that springs *
  From the growing of grass
Are the music of things —
  But are modell'd, alas ! —
Away, then, my dearest,
  O ! hie the away
To springs that lie clearest
  Beneath the moon-ray —
To lone lake that smiles,
  In its dream of deep rest,
At the many star-isles
  That enjewel its breast —
Where wild flowers, creeping,
  Have mingled their shade,
On its margin is sleeping
  Full many a maid —
Some have left the cool glade, and
  Have slept with the bee † —

---

* I met with this idea in an old English tale, which I am now unable to obtain and quote from memory : "The verie essence and, as it were, springe-heade and origine of all musiche is the verie pleasaunte sounde which the trees of the forest do make when they growe."

† The wild bee will not sleep in the shade if there be moonlight.

The rhyme in this verse, as in one about sixty lines before, has an appearance of affectation. It is, however, imitated from Sir W. Scott, or rather from Claude Halero — in whose mouth I admired its effect : —

O ! were there an island,
  Tho' ever so wild
Where woman might smile, and
  No man be beguil'd, etc.

Arouse them my maiden,
  On moorland and lea —
Go! breathe on their slumber,
  All softly in ear,
The musical number
  They slumber'd to hear —
For what can awaken
  An angel so soon,
Whose sleep hath been taken
  Beneath the cold moon,
As the spell which no slumber
  Of witchery may test,
The rhythmical number
  Which lull'd him to rest?"

Spirits in wing, and angels to the view,
A thousand seraphs burst th' Empyrean thro',
Young dreams still hovering on their drowsy flight —
Seraphs in all but "Knowledge," the keen light
That fell, refracted, thro' thy bounds, afar
O Death! from eye of God upon that star:
Sweet was that error — sweeter still that death —
Sweet was that error — ev'n with *us* the breath
Of Science dims the mirror of our joy —
To them 't were the Simoom, and would destroy —
For what (to them) availeth it to know
That Truth is Falsehood — or that Bliss is Woe?

Sweet was their death — with them to die was rife
With the last ecstacy of satiate life —
Beyond that death no immortality —
But sleep that pondereth and is not "to be" —
And there — oh! may my weary spirit dwell —
Apart from Heaven's Eternity — and yet how far from
  Hell! *
What guilty spirit, in what shrubbery dim,
Heard not the stirring summons of that hymn?
But two: they fell: for Heaven no grace imparts
To those who hear not for their beating hearts.
A maiden-angel and her seraph-lover —
O! where (and ye may seek the wide skies over)
Was Love, the blind, near sober Duty known?
Unguided Love hath fallen — 'mid "tears of perfect
    moan." †

---

* With the Arabians there is a medium between Heaven and Hell, where men suffer no punishment, but yet do not attain that tranquil and even happiness which they suppose to be characteristic of heavenly enjoyment.

Un no rompido sueno —
Un dia puro — allegre — libre
Quiera —
Libre de amor — de zelo —
De odio — de esperanza — de rezelo. — *Luis Ponce de Leon.*

Sorrow is not excluded from "Al Aaraaf," but it is that sorrow which the living love to cherish for the dead, and which, in some minds, resembles the delirium of opium. The passionate excitement of Love and the buoyancy of spirit attendant upon intoxication are its less holy pleasures — the price of which, to those souls who make choice of "Al Aaraaf" as the residence after life, is final death and annihilation.

† There be tears of perfect moan
Wept for thee in Helicon. — *Milton.*

He was a goodly spirit — he who fell:
A wanderer by mossy-mantled well —
A gazer on the lights that shine above —
A dreamer in the moonbeam by his love!
What wonder? for each star is eye-like there,
And looks so sweetly down on Beauty's hair —
And they, and ev'ry mossy spring were holy
To his love-haunted heart and melancholy.
The night had found (to him a night of woe)
Upon a mountain crag, young Angelo —
Beetling, it bends athwart the solemn sky,
And scowls on starry worlds that down beneath it lie.
Here sate he with his love — his dark eye bent
With eagle gaze along the firmament:
Now turn'd it upon her — but ever then
It trembled to the orb of EARTH again.

"Ianthe, dearest, see! how dim that ray!
How lovely 't is to look so far away!
She seem'd not thus upon that autumn eve
I left her gorgeous halls — nor mourned to leave.
That eve — that eve — I should remember well —
The sun-ray dropp'd, in Lemnos, with a spell
On th' Arabesque carving of a gilded hall
Wherein I sate, and on the draperied wall —
And on my eyelids — oh the heavy light!
How drowsily it weigh'd them into night!

On flowers, before, and mist, and love they ran
With Persian Saadi in his Gulistan:
But oh that light! — I slumber'd — Death, the while,
Stole o'er my senses in that lovely isle
So softly that no single silken hair
Awoke that slept — or knew that he was there.

"The last spot of Earth's orb I trod upon
Was a proud temple call'd the Parthenon * —
More beauty clung around her column'd wall
Than ev'n thy glowing bosom beats withal,†
And when old Time my wing did disenthral
Thence sprang I — as the eagle from his tower,
And years I left behind me in an hour.
What time upon her airy bounds I hung
One half the garden of her globe was flung
Unrolling as a chart unto my view —
Tenantless cities of the desert too!
Ianthe, beauty crowded on me then,
And half I wish'd to be again of men."

"My Angelo! and why of them to be?
A brighter dwelling-place is here for thee —
And greener fields than in yon world above,
And woman's loveliness — and passionate love."

---

* It was entire in 1687 — the most elevated spot in Athens.

† Shadowing more beauty in their airy brows
Than have the white breasts of the Queen of Love. — *Marlowe.*

"But, list, Ianthe! when the air so soft
Fail'd, as my pennon'd spirit leapt aloft,*
Perhaps my brain grew dizzy — but the world
I left so late was into chaos hurl'd —
Sprang from her station, on the winds apart,
And roll'd, a flame, the fiery Heaven athwart.
Methought, my sweet one, then I ceased to soar,
And fell — not swiftly as I rose before,
But with a downward, tremulous motion thro'
Light, brazen rays, this golden star unto!
Nor long the measure of my falling hours.
For nearest of all stars was thine to ours —
Dread star! that came, amid a night of mirth,
A red Dædalion on the timid Earth.

"We came — and to thy Earth — but not to us
Be given our lady's bidding to discuss:
We came, my love; around, above, below,
Gay fire-fly of the night we come and go,
Nor ask a reason save the angel-nod
*She* grants to us, as granted by her God —
But, Angelo, than thine gray Time unfurl'd
Never his fairy wing o'er fairer world!
Dim was its little disk, and angel eyes
Alone could see the phantom in the skies,

* Pennon — for pinion. — *Milton.*

When first Al Aaraaf knew her course to be
Headlong thitherward o'er the starry sea —
But when its glory swell'd upon the sky,
As glowing Beauty's bust beneath man's eye,
We paus'd before the heritage of men,
And thy star trembled — as doth Beauty then!"

Thus, in discourse, the lovers whiled away [day.
The night that waned and waned and brought no
They fell: for Heaven to them no hope imparts
Who hear not for the beating of their hearts.

---

## TO THE RIVER ——.

FAIR river! in thy bright, clear flow
Of crystal, wandering water,
Thou art an emblem of the glow
Of beauty — the unhidden heart —
The playful maziness of art
In old Alberto's daughter;

But when within thy wave she looks —
Which glistens then, and trembles —
Why, then, the prettiest of brooks
Her worshipper resembles;
For in his heart, as in thy stream,
Her image deeply lies —
His heart which trembles at the beam
Of her soul-searching eyes.

# TAMERLANE.

KIND solace in a dying hour!
  Such, father, is not (now) my theme —
I will not madly deem that power
    Of Earth may shrive me of the sin
    Unearthly pride hath revell'd in —
  I have no time to dote or dream:
You call it hope — that fire of fire!
It is but agony of desire:
If I *can* hope — oh God! I can —
  Its fount is holier — more divine —
I would not call thee fool, old man,
  But such is not a gift of thine.

Know thou the secret of a spirit
  Bow'd from its wild pride into shame.
O yearning heart! I did inherit
  Thy withering portion with the fame,
The searing glory which hath shone
Amid the jewels of my throne,
Halo of Hell! and with a pain
Not Hell shall make me fear again —
O craving heart, for the lost flowers
And sunshine of my summer hours!
The undying voice of that dead time,
With its interminable chime,
Rings, in the spirit of a spell,
Upon thy emptiness — a knell.

I have not always been as now:
The fever'd diadem on my brow
I claim'd and won usurpingly —
Hath not the same fierce heirdom given
Rome to the Cæsar — this to me?
The heritage of a kingly mind,
And a proud spirit which hath striven
Triumphantly with human kind.
On mountain soil I first drew life:
The mists of the Taglay have shed
Nightly their dews upon my head,
And, I believe, the winged strife
And tumult of the headlong air
Have nestled in my very hair.

So late from Heaven — that dew — it fell
('Mid dreams of an unholy night)
Upon me with the touch of Hell,
While the red flashing of the light
From clouds that hung, like banners, o'er,
Appeared to my half-closing eye
The pageantry of monarchy,
And the deep trumpet-thunder's roar
Came hurriedly upon me, telling
Of human battle, where my voice,
My own voice, silly child! — was swelling
(O! how my spirit would rejoice,
And leap within me at the cry)
The battle-cry of Victory!

The rain came down upon my head
  Unshelter'd — and the heavy wind
  Rendered me mad and deaf and blind.
It was but man, I thought, who shed
  Laurels upon me : and the rush —
The torrent of the chilly air
Gurgled within my ear the crush
  Of empires — with the captive's prayer —
The hum of suitors — and the tone
Of flattery 'round a sovereign's throne.

My passions, from that hapless hour,
  Usurp'd a tyranny which men
Have deem'd, since I have reach'd to power,
    My innate nature — be it so :
  But, father, there liv'd one who, then,
Then — in my boyhood — when their fire
    Burn'd with a still intenser glow
(For passion must, with youth, expire)
  E'en *then* who knew this iron heart
  In woman's weakness had a part.

I have no words — alas ! — to tell
The loveliness of loving well !
Nor would I now attempt to trace
The more than beauty of a face
Whose lineaments, upon my mind,
Are — shadows on th' unstable wind :

Thus I remember having dwelt
  Some page of early lore upon,
With loitering eye, till I have felt
The letters — with their meaning — melt
  To fantasies — with none.

O, she was worthy of all love!
  Love — as in infancy was mine —
'T was such as angel minds above
  Might envy; her young heart the shrine
On which my every hope and thought
  Were incense — then a goodly gift,
    For they were childish and upright —
Pure — as her young example taught:
  Why did I leave it, and, adrift,
    Trust to the fire within, for light?

We grew in age — and love — together —
  Roaming the forest and the wild;
My breast her shield in wintry weather —
  And when the friendly sunshine smil'd,
And she would mark the opening skies,
*I* saw no Heaven — but in her eyes.

Young Love's first lesson is — the heart:
  For 'mid that sunshine, and those smiles,
When, from our little cares apart,
  And laughing at her girlish wiles,

I 'd throw me on her throbbing breast,
  And pour my spirit out in tears —
There was no need to speak the rest —
  No need to quiet any fears
Of her — who ask'd no reason why,
But turn'd on me her quiet eye!

Yet *more* than worthy of the love
My spirit struggled with, and strove,
When, on the mountain-peak, alone,
Ambition lent it a new tone —
I had no being — but in thee:
  The world, and all it did contain
In the earth — the air — the sea —
  Its joy — its little lot of pain
That was new pleasure — the ideal,
  Dim vanities of dreams by night —
And dimmer nothings which were real —
  (Shadows — and a more shadowy light!)
Parted upon their misty wings,
    And so, confusedly, became
    Thine image and — a name — a name!
Two separate — yet most intimate things.

I was ambitious — have you known
    The passion, father? You have not:
A cottager, I mark'd a throne
Of half the world as all my own,

And murmur'd at such lowly lot—
But, just like any other dream,
Upon the vapor of the dew
My own had past, did not the beam
Of beauty which did while it thro'
The minute — the hour — the day — oppress
My mind with double loveliness.

We walk'd together on the crown
Of a high mountain which look'd down
Afar from its proud natural towers
Of rock and forest, on the hills —
The dwindled hills! begirt with bowers
And shouting with a thousand rills.

I spoke to her of power and pride,
But mystically — in such guise
That she might deem it nought beside
The moment's converse; in her eyes
I read, perhaps too carelessly,
A mingled feeling with my own;
The flush on her bright cheek, to me
Seem'd to become a queenly throne
Too well that I should let it be
Light in the wilderness alone.

I wrapp'd myself in grandeur then
And donn'd a visionary crown —

Yet it was not that Fantasy
Had thrown her mantle over me —
But that, among the rabble — men,
Lion ambition is chain'd down —
And crouches to a keeper's hand —
Not so in deserts where the grand —
The wild — the terrible conspire
With their own breath to fan his fire.

Look 'round thee now on Samarcand!
Is she not queen of Earth? her pride
Above all cities? in her hand
Their destinies? in all beside
Of glory which the world hath known
Stands she not nobly and alone?
Falling — her veriest stepping-stone
Shall form the pedestal of a throne —
And who her sovereign? Timour — he
Whom the astonished people saw
Striding o'er empires haughtily
A diadem'd outlaw!

O, human love! thou spirit given,
On Earth, of all we hope in Heaven!
Which fall'st into the soul like rain
Upon the Siroc-wither'd plain,
And, failing in thy power to bless,
But leav'st the heart a wilderness!

Idea! which bindest life around
With music of so strange a sound
And beauty of so wild a birth —
Farewell! for I have won the Earth.

When Hope, the eagle that tower'd, could see
  No cliff beyond him in the sky,
His pinions were bent droopingly —
  And homeward turn'd his soften'd eye.
'T was sunset; when the sun will part
There comes a sullenness of heart
To him who still would look upon
The glory of the summer sun.
That soul will hate the ev'ning mist
So often lovely, and will list
To the sound of the coming darkness (known
To those whose spirits harken) as one
Who, in a dream of night, *would* fly
But *cannot* from a danger nigh.

What tho' the moon — the white moon
Shed all the splendor of her noon,
*Her* smile is chilly — and *her* beam,
In that time of dreariness, will seem
(So like you gather in your breath)
A portrait taken after death.
And boyhood is a summer sun
Whose waning is the dreariest one —

For all we live to know is known,
And all we seek to keep hath flown —
Let life, then, as the day-flower, fall
With the noonday beauty — which is all.

I reach'd my home — my home no more —
For all had flown who made it so.
I pass'd from out its mossy door,
And, tho' my tread was soft and low,
A voice came from the threshold stone
Of one whom I had earlier known —
O, I defy thee, Hell, to show
On beds of fire that burn below,
A humbler heart — a deeper woe.

Father, I firmly do believe —
I *know* — for Death who comes for me
From regions of the blest afar,
Where there is nothing to deceive,
Hath left his iron gate ajar,
And rays of truth you cannot see
Are flashing thro' Eternity —
I do believe that Eblis hath
A snare in every human path —
Else how, when in the holy grove,
I wandered of the idol, Love,
Who daily scents his snowy wings
With incense of burnt offerings

From the most unpolluted things,
Whose pleasant bowers are yet so riven
Above with trellis'd rays from Heaven,
No mote may shun — no tiniest fly —
The lightning of his eagle eye —
How was it that Ambition crept,
  Unseen, amid the revels there,
Till growing bold, he laughed and leapt
  In the tangles of Love's very hair?

---

## TO ——.

THE bowers whereat, in dreams, I see
  The wantonest singing birds,
Are lips — and all thy melody
  Of lip-begotten words.

Thine eyes, in Heaven of heart enshrined,
  Then desolately fall,
O God! on my funereal mind
  Like starlight on a pall.

Thy heart — *thy* heart — I wake and sigh,
  And sleep to dream till day
Of the truth that gold can never buy —
  Of the baubles that it may.

## A DREAM.

IN visions of the dark night
  I have dreamed of joy departed —
But a waking dream of life and light
  Hath left me broken-hearted.

Ah! what is not a dream by day
  To him whose eyes are cast
On things around him with a ray
  Turned back upon the past?

That holy dream — that holy dream,
  While all the world were chiding,
Hath cheered me as a lovely beam,
  A lonely spirit guiding.

What though that light, thro' storm and night,
  So trembled from afar —
What could there be more purely bright
  In Truth's day-star?

---

## ROMANCE.

ROMANCE, who loves to nod and sing,
With drowsy head and folded wing,
Among the green leaves as they shake
Far down within some shadowy lake,

To me a painted paroquet
Hath been — a most familiar bird —
Taught me my alphabet to say —
To lisp my very earliest word
While in the wild wood I did lie,
A child — with a most knowing eye.

Of late, eternal Condor years
So shake the very Heaven on high
With tumult as they thunder by,
I have no time for idle cares
Through gazing on the unquiet sky.
And when an hour with calmer wings
Its down upon my spirit flings —
That little time with lyre and rhyme
To while away — forbidden things!
My heart would feel to be a crime
Unless it trembled with the strings.

---

## FAIRY-LAND.

DIM vales — and shadowy floods —
And cloudy-looking woods,
Whose forms we can't discover
For the tears that drip all over:
Huge moons there wax and wane —
Again — again — again —

Every moment of the night —
Forever changing places —
And they put out the star-light
With the breath from their pale faces.
About twelve by the moon-dial
One more filmy than the rest
(A kind which, upon trial,
They have found to be the best)
Comes down — still down — and down
With its centre on the crown
Of a mountain's eminence,
While its wide circumference
In easy drapery falls
Over hamlets, over halls,
Wherever they may be —
O'er the strange woods — o'er the sea —
Over spirits on the wing —
Over every drowsy thing —
And buries them up quite
In a labyrinth of light —
And then, how deep ! — oh, deep
Is the passion of their sleep.
In the morning they arise,
And their moony covering
Is soaring in the skies,
With the tempests as they toss,
Like — almost anything —
Or a yellow Albatross.

They use that moon no more
For the same end as before —
Videlicet a tent —
Which I think extravagant:
Its atomies, however,
Into a shower dissever,
Of which those butterflies,
Of Earth, who seek the skies,
And so come down again
(Never-contented things!)
Have brought a specimen
Upon their quivering wings.

---

## THE LAKE. — TO ——.

IN spring of youth it was my lot
To haunt of the wide world a spot
The which I could not love the less —
So lovely was the loneliness
Of a wild lake, with black rock bound,
And the tall pines that towered around.
But when the Night had thrown her pall
Upon that spot, as upon all,
And the mystic wind went by
Murmuring in melody —
Then — ah, then I would awake
To the terror of the lone lake.

Yet that terror was not fright,
But a tremulous delight —
A feeling not the jewelled mine
Could teach or bribe me to define —
Nor Love — although the Love were thine.

Death was in that poisonous wave,
And its gulf a fitting grave
For him who thence could solace bring
To his lone imagining —
Whose solitary soul could make
An Eden of that dim lake.

---

## SONG.

SAW thee on the bridal day,
When a burning blush came o'er thee,
Though happiness around thee lay,
The world all love before thee:

And in thine eye a kindling light
(Whatever it might be)
Was all on Earth my aching sight
Of Loveliness could see.

That blush, perhaps, was maiden shame —
As such it well may pass —
Though its glow hath raised a fiercer flame
In the breast of him, alas!

Who saw thee on that bridal day,
  When that deep blush *would* come o'er thee,
Though happiness around thee lay,
  The world all love before thee.

---

## TO M. L. S——.

OF all who hail thy presence as the morning —
  Of all to whom thine absence is the night —
    The blotting utterly from out high heaven
The sacred sun — of all who, weeping, bless thee
Hourly for hope — for life — ah! above all,
For the resurrection of deep-buried faith
In Truth — in Virtue — in Humanity —
Of all who, on Despair's unhallowed bed
Lying down to die, have suddenly arisen
At thy soft-murmured words, "Let there be light!"
At the soft-murmured words that were fulfilled
In the seraphic glancing of thine eyes —
Of all who owe thee most — whose gratitude
Nearest resembles worship — oh, remember
The truest — the most fervently devoted,
And think that these weak lines are written by him —
By him who, as he pens them, thrills to think
His spirit is communing with an angel's.

# THE POETIC PRINCIPLE.

# THE POETIC PRINCIPLE.

In speaking of the Poetic Principle, I have no design to be either thorough or profound. While discussing, very much at random, the essentiality of what we call Poetry, my principal purpose will be to cite for consideration some few of those minor English or American poems which best suit my own taste, or which, upon my own fancy, have left the most definite impression. By "minor poems" I mean, of course, poems of little length. And here, in the beginning, permit me to say a few words in regard to a somewhat peculiar principle, which, whether rightfully or wrongfully, has always had its influence in my own critical estimate of the poem. I hold that a long poem does not exist. I maintain that the phrase "a long poem" is simply a flat contradiction in terms.

I need scarcely observe that a poem deserves its title only inasmuch as it excites by elevating the soul. The value of the poem is in the ratio of this elevating excitement. But all excitements are, through a psychal necessity, transient. That degree of excitement which would entitle a poem to be so called at all cannot be sustained throughout a composition of any great length. After the lapse of half an hour, at the very utmost, it flags, fails, a revulsion ensues; and then the poem is, in effect and in fact, no longer such.

There are, no doubt, many who have found difficulty in reconciling the critical dictum that the "Paradise Lost" is to be devoutly admired throughout with the absolute impossibility of maintaining for it, during perusal, the amount of enthusiasm which that critical dictum would demand. This great work, in fact, is to be regarded as poetical only when, losing sight of that vital requisite in all works of art, unity, we view it merely as a series of minor poems. If, to preserve its unity, — its totality of effect or impression, — we read it (as would be necessary) at a single sitting, the result is but a constant alternation of excitement and depression. After a passage of what we feel to be true poetry, there follows, inevitably, a passage of platitude which no critical pre-judgment can force us to admire; but if, upon completing the work, we read it again, omitting the first book, — that is to say, commencing with the second, — we shall be surprised at now finding that admirable which we before condemned, that damnable which we had previously so much admired. It follows from all this that the ultimate, aggregate, or absolute effect of even the best epic under the sun is a nullity: and this is precisely the fact.

In regard to the Iliad, we have, if not positive proof, at least very good reason, for believing it intended as a series of lyrics; but granting the epic intention, I can say only that the work is based in an imperfect sense of art. The modern epic is of the suppositious ancient model, but an inconsiderate and blindfold imitation. But the day of these artistic anomalies is over. If, at any time, any very long poem *were* popular in reality,— which I doubt,—it is at least clear that no very long poem will ever be popular again.

That the extent of a poetical work is, *ceteris paribus*, the measure of its merit, seems undoubtedly, when we thus state it, a proposition sufficiently absurd; yet we are indebted for it to the Quarterly Reviews. Surely there can be nothing in mere *size*, abstractly considered, there can be nothing in mere *bulk*, so far as a volume is concerned, which has so continuously elicited admiration from these saturnine pamphlets! A mountain, to be sure, by the mere sentiment of physical magnitude which it conveys, *does* impress us with a sense of the sublime; but no man is impressed after *this* fashion by the material grandeur of even "The Columbiad." Even the Quarterlies have not instructed us to be so impressed by it. *As yet*, they have not *insisted* on our estimating Lamartine by the cubic foot, or Pollock by the pound; but what else are we to *infer* from their continual prating about "sustained effort"? If by "sustained effort" any little gentleman has accomplished an epic, let us frankly commend him for the effort, — if this indeed be a thing commendable, — but let us forbear praising the epic on the effort's account.

It is to be hoped that common-sense, in the time to come, will prefer deciding upon a work of art rather by the impression it makes, by the effect it produces, than by the time it took to impress the effect, or by the amount of "sustained effort" which had been found necessary in effecting the impression. The fact is, that perseverance is one thing and genius quite another, nor can all the Quarterlies in Christendom confound them. By and by this proposition, with many which I have been just urging, will be received as self-evident. In the mean time, by being generally condemned as falsities, they will not be essentially damaged as truths.

On the other hand, it is clear that a poem may be improperly brief. Undue brevity degenerates into mere epigrammatism. A *very* short poem, while now and then producing a brilliant or vivid, never produces a profound or enduring effect. There must be the steady pressing down of the stamp upon the wax. De Béranger has wrought innumerable things, pungent and spirit-stirring; but, in general, they have been too imponderous to stamp themselves deeply into the public attention; and thus, as so many feathers of fancy, have been blown aloft only to be whistled down the wind.

A remarkable instance of the effect of undue brevity in depressing a poem, — in keeping it out of the popular view, is afforded by the following exquisite little serenade: —

I arise from dreams of thee
  In the first sweet sleep of night,
When the winds are breathing low
  And the stars are shining bright.
I arise from dreams of thee,
  And a spirit in my feet
Has led me — who knows how? —
  To thy chamber-window, sweet!

The wandering airs they faint
  On the dark, the silent stream;
The champak odors fail
  Like sweet thoughts in a dream;
The nightingale's complaint,
  It dies upon her heart,
As I must die on thine,
  Oh, beloved, as thou art!

Oh, lift me from the grass!
  I die, I faint, I fail!
Let thy love in kisses rain
  On my lips and eyelids pale.

My cheek is cold and white, alas!
  My heart beats loud and fast:
Oh! press it close to thine again,
  Where it will break at last.

Very few, perhaps, are familiar with these lines, yet no less a poet than Shelley is their author. Their warm yet delicate and ethereal imagination will be appreciated by all; but by none so thoroughly as by him who has himself arisen from sweet dreams of one beloved to bathe in the aromatic air of a southern midsummer night.

One of the finest poems by Willis — the very best, in my opinion, which he has ever written — has, no doubt through this same defect of undue brevity, been kept back from its proper position, not less in the critical than in the popular view.

The shadows lay along Broadway,
  'T was near the twilight tide,
And slowly there a lady fair
  Was walking in her pride.
Alone walked she, but viewlessly
  Walked spirits at her side.

Peace charmed the street beneath her feet,
  And Honor charmed the air,

And all astir looked kind on her,
  And called her good as fair;
For all God ever gave to her
  She kept with chary care.

She kept with care her beauties rare
  From lovers warm and true,
For her heart was cold to all but gold,
  And the rich came not to woo:
But honored well are charms to sell
  If priests the selling do.

Now walking there was one more fair,—
  A slight girl, lily-pale;
And she had unseen company
  To make the spirit quail:
'Twixt Want and Scorn she walked forlorn,
  And nothing could avail.

No mercy now can clear her brow
  For this world's peace to pray;
For, as love's wild prayer dissolved in air,
  Her woman's heart gave way!—
But the sin forgiven by Christ in Heaven
  By man is cursed alway!

In this composition we find it difficult to recognize the Willis who has written so many mere "verses of society." The lines are not only richly ideal, but full of energy, while they breathe an earnestness, an evident sincerity of sentiment, for which we look in vain throughout all the other works of this author.

While the epic mania — while the idea that to merit, in poetry, prolixity is indispensable — has, for some years past, been gradually dying out of the public mind by mere dint of its own absurdity, we find it succeeded by a heresy too palpably false to be long tolerated, but one which, in the brief period it has already endured, may be said to have accomplished more in the corruption of our poetical literature than all its other enemies combined. I allude to the heresy of *The Didactic*. It has been assumed, tacitly and avowedly, directly and indirectly, that the ultimate object of all poetry is truth. Every poem, it is said, should inculcate a moral; and by this moral is the poetical merit of the work to be adjudged. We Americans especially have patronized this happy idea; and we Bostonians, very especially, have developed it in full. We have taken it into our heads that to write a poem simply for the poem's sake, and to acknowledge such to have been our design, would be to confess ourselves radically wanting in the true poetic dignity and force; but the simple fact is that, would we but permit ourselves to look into our own souls, we should immediately there discover that under the sun there neither exists nor *can* exist any work more thoroughly dignified, more supremely noble, than this very poem; this poem *per se;* this poem which is a poem and nothing more; this poem written solely for the poem's sake.

With as deep a reverence for the True as ever inspired the bosom of man, I would nevertheless limit, in some measure, its modes of inculcation. I would limit, to enforce them. I would not enfeeble them by dissipation. The demands of Truth are severe. She has no sympathy with the myrtles. All *that* which is so indispensable in Song is precisely all *that* with which *she* has nothing whatever to do. It is but making her a flaunting paradox to wreathe her in gems and flowers. In enforcing a truth, we need severity rather than efflorescence of language. We must be simple, precise, terse; we must be cool, calm, unimpassioned; in a word, we must be in that mood which, as nearly as possible, is the exact converse of the poetical. *He* must be blind indeed who does not perceive the radical and chasmal differences between the truthful and the poetical modes of inculcation. He must be theory-mad beyond redemption who, in spite of these differences, shall still persist in attempting to reconcile the obstinate oils and waters of Poetry and Truth.

Dividing the world of mind into its three most immediately obvious distinctions, we have the Pure Intellect, Taste, and the Moral Sense. I place Taste in the middle because it is just this position which, in the mind, it occupies. It holds intimate relations with either extreme, but from the Moral Sense is separated by so faint a difference that Aristotle has not hesitated to place some of its operations among the virtues themselves. Nevertheless, we find the *offices* of the trio marked with a sufficient distinction. Just as the Intellect concerns itself with Truth, so Taste informs us of the Beautiful, while the Moral Sense is regardful of Duty. Of this latter, while Conscience teaches the obligation, and Reason the expediency, Taste contents herself with displaying the charms; waging war upon Vice solely on the ground of her deformity, her disproportion, her animosity to the fitting, to the appropriate, to the harmonious — in a word, to Beauty.

An immortal instinct, deep within the spirit of man, is thus, plainly, a sense of the Beautiful. This it is which administers to his delight in the manifold forms and sounds and odors and sentiments amid which he exists. And just as the lily is repeated in the lake, or the eyes of Amaryllis in the mirror, so is the mere oral or written repetition of these forms and sounds and colors and odors and sentiments a duplicate source of delight. But this mere repetition is not poetry. He who shall simply sing, with however glowing enthusiasm or with however vivid a truth of description, of the sights and sounds and odors and colors and sentiments which greet *him* in common with all mankind, —

he, I say, has yet failed to prove his divine title. There is still a something in the distance which he has been unable to attain. We have still a thirst unquenchable, to allay which he has not shown us the crystal springs. This thirst belongs to the immortality of man. It is at once a consequence and an indication of his perennial existence. It is the desire of the moth for the star. It is no mere appreciation of the beauty before us, but a wild effort to reach the beauty above. Inspired by an ecstatic prescience of the glories beyond the grave, we struggle, by multiform combinations among the things and thoughts of time, to attain a portion of that loveliness whose very elements, perhaps, appertain to eternity alone. And thus when by poetry — or when by music, the most entrancing of the poetic moods — we find ourselves melted into tears, we weep then, not, as the Abbate Gravina supposes, through excess of pleasure, but through a certain petulant, impatient sorrow at our inability to grasp *now*, wholly, here on earth, at once and forever, those divine and rapturous joys, of which *through* the poem or *through* the music, we attain to but brief and indeterminate glimpses.

The struggle to apprehend the supernal loveliness, this struggle, on the part of souls fittingly constituted, has given to the world all that which it (the world) has ever been enabled at once to understand and *to feel* as poetic.

The poetic sentiment, of course, may develop itself in various modes,—in painting, in sculpture, in architecture, in the dance, very especially in music, and very peculiarly, and with a wide field, in the composition of the landscape garden. Our present theme, however, has regard only to its manifestation in words. And here let me speak briefly on the topic of rhythm. Contenting myself with the certainty that music, in its various modes of metre, rhythm, and rhyme, is of so vast a moment in poetry as never to be wisely rejected, is so vitally important an adjunct that he is simply silly who declines its assistance, I will not now pause to maintain its absolute essentiality. It is in music, perhaps, that the soul most nearly attains the great end for which, when inspired by the poetic sentiment, it struggles, — the creation of supernal beauty. It *may* be, indeed, that here this sublime end is, now and then, attained, *in fact.* We are often made to feel, with a shivering delight, that from an earthly harp are stricken notes which *cannot* have been unfamiliar to the angels. And thus there can be little doubt that in the union of poetry with music in its popular sense, we shall find the widest field for the poetic development. The old bards and minnesingers had advantages which we do not possess; and Thomas Moore, singing his own songs, was, in the most legitimate manner, perfecting them as poems.

To recapitulate, then: — I would define, in brief, the

poetry of words as *the rhythmical creation of beauty.* Its sole arbiter is Taste. With the intellect or with the conscience, it has only collateral relations. Unless incidentally, it has no concern whatever either with Duty or with Truth.

A few words, however, in explanation. *That* pleasure which is at once the most pure, the most elevating, and the most intense, is derived, I maintain, from the contemplation of the Beautiful. In the contemplation of Beauty, we alone find it possible to attain this pleasurable elevation or excitement *of the soul* which we recognize as the poetic sentiment, and which is so easily distinguished from Truth, which is the satisfaction of the Reason, or from Passion, which is the excitement of the heart. I make Beauty, therefore, using the word as inclusive of the sublime, — I make Beauty the province of the poem, simply because it is an obvious rule of art that effects should be made to spring as directly as possible from their causes, — no one as yet having been weak enough to deny that the peculiar elevation in ques- is at least *most readily* attainable in the poem. It by no means follows, however, that the incitements of Passion or the precepts of Duty, or even the lessons of Truth, may not be introduced into a poem, and with advantage; for they may subserve, incidentally, in various ways, the general purposes of the work: but the true artist will always contrive to tone them down in proper subjection to that *Beauty* which is the atmosphere and the real essence of the poem.

I cannot better introduce the few poems which I shall present for your consideration than by the citation of the pröem to Mr. Longfellow's "Waif."

> The day is done, and the darkness
>   Falls from the wings of Night,
> As a feather is wafted downward
>   From an eagle in his flight.
>
> I see the lights of the village
>   Gleam through the rain and the mist,
> And a feeling of sadness comes o'er me
>   That my soul cannot resist, —
>
> A feeling of sadness and longing,
>   That is not akin to pain,
> And resembles sorrow only
>   As the mist resembles rain.
>
> Come, read to me some poem,
>   Some simple and heartfelt lay,
> That shall soothe this restless feeling,
>   And banish the thoughts of day.
>
> Not from the grand old masters,
>   Not from the bards sublime,
> Whose distant footsteps echo
>   Through the corridors of Time;

For, like strains of martial music,
  Their mighty thoughts suggest
Life's endless toil and endeavor;
  And to-night I long for rest.

Read from some humbler poet,
  Whose songs gushed from his heart
As showers from the clouds of summer
  Or tears from the eyelids start;

Who, through long days of labor
  And nights devoid of ease,
Still heard in his soul the music
  Of wonderful melodies.

Such songs have power to quiet
  The restless pulse of care,
And come like the benediction
  That follows after prayer.

Then read from the treasured volume
  The poem of thy choice,
And lend to the rhyme of the poet
  The beauty of thy voice.

And the night shall be filled with music,
  And the cares that infest the day
Shall fold their tents, like the Arabs,
  And as silently steal away.

With no great range of imagination, these lines have been justly admired for their delicacy of expression. Some of the images are very effective. Nothing can be better than

——————— The bards sublime,  
Whose distant footsteps echo  
Down the corridors of Time.

The idea of the last quartrain is also very effective. The poem, on the whole, however, is chiefly to be admired for the graceful *insouciance* of its metre, so well in accordance with the character of the sentiments, and especially for the *ease* of the general manner. This "ease," or naturalness, in a literary style, it has long been the fashion to regard as ease in appearance alone, — as a point of really difficult attainment. But not so: a natural manner is difficult only to him who should never meddle with it, — to the unnatural. It is but the result of writing with the understanding, or with the instinct, that *the tone*, in composition, should always be that which the mass of mankind would adopt, and must perpetually vary, of course, with the occasion. The author who, after the fashion of "The North American Review," should be, upon *all* occasions, merely "quiet," must necessarily, upon *many* occasions, be simply silly or stupid; and has no more right to be considered "easy" or "natural," than a cockney exquisite, or than the sleeping Beauty in the wax-works.

Among the minor poems of Bryant, none has so much impressed me as the one which he entitles "June." I quote only a portion of it: —

There, through the long, long summer hours
        The golden light should lie,
And thick, young herbs and groups of flowers
        Stand in their beauty by.
The oriole should build and tell
His love-tale, close beside my cell;
        The idle butterfly
Should rest him there, and there be heard
The housewife-bee and humming-bird.

And what if cheerful shouts, at noon,
        Come, from the village sent,
Or songs of maids, beneath the moon,
        With fairy laughter blent?
And what if, in the evening light,
Betrothéd lovers walk in sight
        Of my low monument?
I would the lovely scene around
Might know no sadder sight nor sound.

I know, I know I should not see
        The season's glorious show,
Nor would its brightness shine for me,
        Nor its wild music flow;

But if around my place of sleep,
The friends I love should come to weep,
They might not haste to go.
Soft airs, and song, and light, and bloom,
Should keep them lingering by my tomb.

These to their softened hearts should bear
The thought of what has been,
And speak of one who cannot share
The gladness of the scene ;
Whose part in all the pomp that fills
The circuit of the summer hills,
Is — that his grave is green ;
And deeply would their hearts rejoice
To hear again his living voice.

The rhythmical flow here is even voluptuous — nothing could be more melodious. The poem has always affected me in a remarkable manner. The intense melancholy which seems to well up, perforce, to the surface of all the poet's cheerful sayings about his grave, we find thrilling us to the soul, while there is the truest poetic elevation in the thrill. The impression left is one of a pleasurable sadness. And if, in the remaining compositions which I shall introduce to you, there be more or less of a similar tone always apparent, let me remind you that (how or why we know not) this certain taint of sadness is inseparably connected with all the higher manifestations of true beauty. It is, nevertheless,

A feeling of sadness and longing
  That is not akin to pain,
And resembles sorrow only
  As the mist resembles the rain

The taint of which I speak is clearly perceptible even in a poem so full of brilliancy and spirit as the "Health" of Edward Coate Pinkney: —

I fill this cup to one made up
  Of loveliness alone,
A woman, of her gentle sex
  The seeming paragon;
To whom the better elements
  And kindly stars have given
A form so fair that, like the air
  'T is less of earth than heaven.

Her every tone is music's own,
  Like those of morning birds,
And something more than melody
  Dwells ever in her words;
The coinage of her heart are they,
  And from her lips each flows
As one may see the burden'd bee
  Forth issue from the rose.

Affections are as thoughts to her,
  The measures of her hours ;
Her feelings have the fragrancy,
  The freshness of young flowers ;
And lovely passions, changing oft,
  So fill her, she appears
The image of themselves by turns, —
  The idol of past years !

Of her bright face one glance will trace
  A picture on the brain,
And of her voice in echoing hearts
  A sound must long remain ;
But memory, such as mine of her,
  So very much endears,
When death is nigh my latest sigh
  Will not be life's, but hers.

I fill'd this cup to one made up
  Of loveliness alone,
A woman, of her gentle sex
  The seeming paragon.
Her health ! and would on earth there stood
  Some more of such a frame,
That life might be all poetry,
  And weariness a name.

It was the misfortune of Mr. Pinckney to have been born too far south. Had he been a New Englander, it is probable that he would have been ranked as the first of American lyrists by that magnanimous cabal which has so long controlled the destinies of American Letters in conducting the thing called "The North American Review." The poem just cited is especially beautiful; but the poetic elevation which it induces, we must refer chiefly to our sympathy in the poet's enthusiasm. We pardon his hyperboles for the evident earnestness with which they are uttered.

It was by no means my design, however, to expatiate upon the *merits* of what I should read you. These will necessarily speak for themselves. Boccalini, in his "Advertisements from Parnassus," tells us that Zoilus once presented Apollo a very caustic criticism upon a very admirable book, whereupon the god asked him for the beauties of the work. He replied that he only busied himself about the errors. On hearing this, Apollo, handing him a sack of unwinnowed wheat, bade him pick out *all the chaff* for his reward.

Now this fable answers very well as a hit at the critics; but I am by no means sure that the god was in the right. I am by no means certain that the true limits of the critical duty are not grossly misunderstood. Excellence, in a poem especially, may be considered in the light of an axiom, which need only be properly *put* to become self-evident. It is *not* excellence if it require to be demonstrated as such: and thus, to point out too particularly the merits of a work of art is to admit that they are *not* merits altogether.

Among the "Melodies" of Thomas Moore, is one whose distinguished character as a poem proper, seems to have been singularly left out of view. I allude to his lines beginning "Come, rest in this bosom." The intense energy of their expression is not surpassed by anything in Byron. There are two of the lines in which a sentiment is conveyed that embodies the *all in all* of the divine passion of love, — a sentiment which, perhaps, has found its echo in more, and in more passionate human hearts, than any other single sentiment ever embodied in words: —

Come, rest in this bosom, my own stricken deer,
Though the herd have fled from thee, thy home is still
here;
Here still is the smile that no cloud can o'ercast,
And a heart and a hand all thy own to the last.

Oh! what was love made for, if 't is not the same
Through joy and through torment, through glory and
shame?
I know not, I ask not, if guilt 's in that heart:
I but know that I love thee, whatever thou art.

Thou hast call'd me thy angel in moments of bliss,
And thy angel I 'll be, 'mid the horrors of this, —
Through the furnace, unshrinking, thy steps to pursue,
And shield thee, and save thee, — or perish there too!

It has been the fashion of late days to deny Moore imagination, while granting him fancy, — a distinction originating with Coleridge, than whom no man more fully comprehended the great powers of Moore. The fact is that the fancy of this poet so far predominates over all his other faculties, and over the fancy of all other men, as to have induced, very naturally, the idea that he is fanciful *only*. But never was there a greater mistake, never was a grosser wrong done the fame of a true poet. In the compass of the English language I can call to mind no poem more profoundly, more weirdly *imaginative*, in the best sense, than the lines commencing "I would I were by that dim lake," which are the composition of Thomas Moore. I regret that I am unable to remember them.

One of the noblest — and, speaking of fancy, one of the most singularly fanciful of modern poets — was Thomas Hood. His "Fair Ines" had always, for me, an inexpressible charm: —

Oh, saw ye not Fair Ines?
She 's gone into the West,
To dazzle when the sun is down,
And rob the world of rest.

She took our daylight with her,
  The smiles that we love best,
With morning blushes on her cheek
  And pearls upon her breast.

Oh, turn again, fair Ines,
  Before the fall of night,
For fear the moon should shine alone,
  And stars unrivall'd bright:
And blessed will the lover be
  That walks beneath their light,
And breathes the love against thy cheek
  I dare not even write!

Would I had been, fair Ines,
  That gallant cavalier
Who rode so gayly by thy side,
  And whispered thee so near!
Were there no bonny dames at home,
  Or no true lovers here,
That he should cross the seas to win
  The dearest of the dear?

I saw thee, lovely Ines,
  Descend along the shore,
With a band of noble gentlemen,
  And banners wav'd before;

And gentle youth and maidens gay,
  And snowy plumes they wore;
It would have been a beauteous dream,
  — If it had been no more!

Alas, alas, fair Ines!
  She went away with song,
With Music waiting on her steps,
  And shoutings of the throng;
But some were sad and felt no mirth,
  But only Music's wrong,
In sounds that sang Farewell, Farewell,
  To her you 've loved so long.

Farewell, farewell, fair Ines!
  That vessel never bore
So fair a lady on its deck,
  Nor danced so light before.
Alas for pleasure on the sea
  And sorrow on the shore!
The smile that blest one lover's heart
  Has broken many more!

"The Haunted House," by the same author, is one of the truest poems ever written, one of the *truest*, one of the most unexceptionable, one of the most thoroughly artistic, both in its theme and in its execution. It is, moreover, powerfully ideal, imaginative. I regret that its length renders it unsuitable for the purposes of this Lecture. In place of it, permit me to offer the universally appreciated "Bridge of Sighs":—

One more Unfortunate,
Weary of breath,
Rashly importunate,
Gone to her death.

Take her up tenderly,
Lift her with care,—
Fashion'd so slenderly,
Young, and so fair!

Look at her garments,
Clinging like cerements;
Whilst the wave constantly
Drips from her clothing.
Take her up instantly,
Loving, not loathing.—

Touch her not scornfully,
Think of her mournfully,
Gently and humanly;
Not of the stains of her,
All that remains of her
Now, is pure womanly.

Make no deep scrutiny
Into her mutiny
Rash and undutiful;
Past all dishonor,
Death has left on her
Only the beautiful.

Still, for all slips of hers,
One of Eve's family,
Wipe those poor lips of hers,
Oozing so clammily;
Loop up her tresses
Escaped from the comb,
Her fair auburn tresses,
Whilst wonderment guesses
Where was her home?

Who was her father?
Who was her mother?
Had she a sister?
Had she a brother?
Or was there a dearer one
Still, and a nearer one
Yet, than all other?

Alas! for the rarity
Of Christian charity
Under the sun!

Oh, it was pitiful!
Near a whole city full,
Home she had none.

Sisterly, brotherly,
Fatherly, motherly
Feelings had changed;
Love, by harsh evidence,
Thrown from its eminence;
Even God's providence
Seeming estranged.

Where the lamps quiver
So far in the river,
With many a light
From window and casement,
From garret to basement,
She stood, with amazement,
Houseless by night.

The bleak wind of March
Made her tremble and shiver,
But not the dark arch,
Or the black flowing river:
Mad from life's history,
Glad to death's mystery
Swift to be hurl'd —
Anywhere, anywhere
Out of the world!

In she plunged boldly,
No matter how coldly
The rough river ran, —
Over the brink of it,
Picture it, think of it,
Dissolute man!
Lave in it, drink of it,
Then, if you can!

Take her up tenderly,
Lift her with care, —
Fashion'd so slenderly,
Young, and so fair!

Ere her limbs frigidly
Stiffen too rigidly,
Decently, — kindly, —
Smooth and compose them;
And her eyes, close them,
Staring so blindly!

Dreadfully staring
Through muddy impurity,
As when with the daring
Last look of despairing
Fixed on futurity.

Perishing gloomily,
Spurred by contumely,

Cold inhumanity,
Burning insanity,
Into her rest.
Cross her hands humbly,
As if praying dumbly,
Over her breast!
Owning her weakness,
Her evil behavior,
And leaving, with meekness,
Her sins to her Saviour!

The vigor of this poem is no less remarkable than its pathos. The versification, although carrying the fanciful to the very verge of the fantastic, is nevertheless admirably adapted to the wild insanity which is the thesis of the poem.

Among the minor poems of Lord Byron is one which has never received from the critics the praise which it undoubtedly deserves: —

Though the day of my destiny 's over,
 And the star of my fate hath declined,
Thy soft heart refused to discover
 The faults which so many could find;
Though thy soul with my grief was acquainted,
 It shrunk not to share it with me,
And the love which my spirit hath painted
 It never hath found but in *thee.*

Then when nature around me is smiling,
  The last smile which answers to mine,
I do not believe it beguiling,
  Because it reminds me of thine;
And when winds are at war with the ocean,
  As the breasts I believed in with me,
If their billows excite an emotion,
  It is that they bear me from *thee.*

Though the rock of my last hope is shivered,
  And its fragments are sunk in the wave,
Though I feel that my soul is delivered
  To pain — it shall not be its slave.
There is many a pang to pursue me:
  They may crush, but they shall not contemn;
They may torture, but shall not subdue me:
  'T is of *thee* that I think — not of them.

Though human, thou didst not deceive me,
  Though woman, thou didst not forsake,
Though loved, thou forborest to grieve me,
  Though slandered, thou never couldst shake;
Though trusted, thou didst not disclaim me,
  Though parted, it was not to fly,
Though watchful, 't was not to defame me,
  Nor mute, that the world might belie.

Yet I blame not the world, nor despise it,
  Nor the war of the many with one:
If my soul was not fitted to prize it,
  'T was folly not sooner to shun;
And if dearly that error hath cost me,
  And more than I once could foresee,
I have found that, whatever it lost me,
  It could not deprive me of *thee.*

From the wreck of the past, which hath perished,
  Thus much I at least may recall,
It hath taught me that which I most cherished,
  Deserved to be dearest of all:
In the desert a fountain is springing,
  In the wide waste there still is a tree,
And a bird in the solitude singing,
  Which speaks to my spirit of *thee.*

Although the rhythm, here, is one of the most difficult, the versification could scarcely be improved. No nobler *theme* ever engaged the pen of poet. It is the soul-elevating idea that no man can consider himself entitled to complain of fate, while in his adversity he still retains the unwavering love of woman.

From Alfred Tennyson — although in perfect sincerity I regard him as the noblest poet that ever lived — I have left myself time to cite only a very brief specimen. I call him and *think* him the noblest of poets, — *not* because the impressions he produces are, at *all* times, the most profound; *not* because the poetical excitement which he induces is, at *all* times, the most intense; but because it is, at all times, the most ethereal, in other words, the most elevating and the most pure. No poet is so little of the earth, earthy. What I am about to read is from his last long poem, "The Princess":—

Tears, idle tears, I know not what they mean!
Tears from the depth of some divine despair
Rise in the heart and gather to the eyes,
In looking on the happy Autumn fields,
And thinking of the days that are no more.

Fresh as the first beam glittering on a sail
That brings our friends up from the underworld,
Sad as the last which reddens over one
That sinks with all we love below the verge,—
So sad, so fresh, the days that are no more.

Ah! sad and strange as in dark summer dawns
The earliest pipe of half-awaken'd birds
To dying ears, when unto dying eyes
The casement slowly grows a glimmering square,—
So sad, so strange, the days that are no more.

Dear as remember'd kisses after death,
And sweet as those by hopeless fancy feign'd

On lips that are for others; deep as love,
Deep as first love, and wild with all regret.
O Death in Life! the days that are no more.

Thus, although in a very cursory and imperfect manner, I have endeavored to convey to you my conception of the Poetic Principle. It has been my purpose to suggest that, while this principle itself is, strictly and simply, the human aspiration for supernal beauty, the manifestation of the principle is always found in *an elevating excitement of the soul*, quite independent of that passion which is the intoxication of the heart, or of that truth which is the satisfaction of the reason; for, in regard to passion, alas! its tendency is to degrade rather than to elevate the soul. Love, on the contrary, —Love, the true, the divine Eros, the Uranian as distinguished from the Dionæan Venus,—is unquestionably the purest and truest of all poetical themes. And in regard to Truth, if, to be sure, through the attainment of a truth we are led to perceive a harmony where none was apparent before, we experience at once the true poetical effect; but this effect is referrible to the harmony alone, and not in the least degree to the truth which merely served to render the harmony manifest.

We shall reach, however, more immediately a distinct conception of what the true poetry is by mere reference to a few of the simple elements which induce in the poet himself the true poetical effect. He recognizes the ambrosia which nourishes his soul, in the bright orbs that shine in Heaven, in the volutes of the flower, in the clustering of low shrubberies, in the waving of the grain-fields, in the slanting of tall, eastern trees, in the blue distance of mountains, in the grouping of clouds, in the twinkling of half-hidden brooks, in the gleaming of silver rivers, in the repose of sequestered lakes, in the star-mirroring depths of lonely wells. He perceives it in the songs of birds, in the harp of Æolus, in the sighing of the night-wind, in the repining voice of the forest, in the surf that complains to the shore, in the fresh breath of the woods, in the scent of the violet, in the voluptuous perfume of the hyacinth, in the suggestive odor that comes to him, at eventide, from far-distant, undiscovered islands, over dim oceans, illimitable and unexplored. He owns it in all noble thoughts, in all unworldly motives, in all holy impulses, in all chivalrous, generous, and self-sacrificing deeds. He feels it in the beauty of woman, — in the grace of her step, in the lustre of her eye, in the melody of her voice, in her soft laughter, in her sigh, in the harmony of the rustling of her robes. He deeply feels it in her winning endearments, in her burning enthusiasms, in her gentle charities, in her meek and devotional endurances; but above all, ah! far above all, he kneels to it, he worships it in the faith, in the purity, in the strength, in the altogether divine majesty of her *love.*

Let me conclude by the recitation of yet another brief poem, one very different in character from any that I have before quoted. It is by Motherwell, and is called "The Song of the Cavalier." With our modern and altogether rational ideas of the absurdity and impiety of warfare, we are not precisely in that frame of mind best adapted to sympathize with the sentiments, and thus to appreciate the real excellence of the poem. To do this fully, we must identify ourselves, in fancy, with the soul of the old cavalier.

Then mounte, then mounte, brave gallants all,
  And don your helmes amaine!
Deathe's couriers, Fame and Honor, call
  Us to the field againe.
No shrewish teares shall fill our eye
  When the sword-hilt 's in our hand;
Heart-whole we 'll part, and no whit sighe
  For the fayrest of the land.
Let piping swaine and craven wight
  Thus weepe and puling crye:
Our business is like men to fight,
  And hero-like to die.

THE END.

www.ingramcontent.com/pod-product-compliance
Lightning Source LLC
LaVergne TN
LVHW011224110826
845150LV00006B/1535

* 9 7 8 1 4 2 5 5 1 5 8 4 3 *